MALTA LOOKS TO US FOR HELP. WE SHALL NOT FAIL THEM.

The garrison and people of Malta, who have been defending their island so gallantly against incessant attacks by the German and Italian air forces, are in urgent need of replenishments of food and military supplies. These we are taking to them and I ask that every officer in the convoy and its escort will do his utmost to ensure that they reach Malta safely. You may be sure that the enemy will do all in his power to prevent the convoy getting through and it will require every exertion on our part to see that he fails in his attempt. During the next few days all ships will be in the first and second degree of readiness for long periods. When you are on watch be especially vigilant and alert, and, for that reason, when you are off duty, get all the sleep you can. Every one of us must give of his best. Malta looks to us for help. We shall not fail them.

VICE-ADMIRAL E.N. SYFRET,
who commanded Operation Pedestal,
sent this signal to all the ships.

GOD SPEED AND GOOD LUCK

Before you start on this operation , the First Sea Lord and I are anxious you should know how grateful the Board of Admiralty are to you for undertaking this difficult task.

Malta has for some time been in great danger. It is imperative that she should be kept supplied. These are her critical months and we cannot fail her.

She has stood up to the most violent attacks from the air that have ever been made and now she needs your help in continuing the battle.

Her courage is worthy of yours.

We know that Admiral Syfret will do all he can to complete the operation with success and that you will stand by him according to the splendid traditions of the Merchant Navy.

We wish you all "God Speed and Good Luck".

A.V. ALEXANDER,
First Lord of the Admiralty
July 23, 1942

Front Cover:
This dramatic painting of H.M.S. *Ledbury* rescuing survivors of the *Waimarama* is by John Hamilton, one of the leading painters of the Second World War. His paintings number over 200 and are at the National Maritime Museum, Greenwich, and the U.S. Navy Art Collection in Washington. Over 170 of his superb paintings have been published, supported by a detailed text, in "War at Sea" in 1986, now itself a collectors' item. Hamilton died in 1993, aged 75. (Imperial War Museums Collection)

Previous page:
The embossed figure of *Santa Marija*, designed by the architect Michael Sandle, for the Siege of Malta 10-ton bell for the memorial overlooking the entrance to Grand Harbour. It symbolizes the arrival of the Pedestal Convoy in August 1942. The Siege Bell Memorial was unveiled by Dr. Vincent Tabone, President of Malta, and Queen Elizabeth II on 22 May, 1992.

John A. Mizzi

OPERATION
PEDESTAL

midsea BOOKS

First published in Malta by
Midsea Books Ltd
6 Strait Street, Valletta, Malta
www.midseabooks.com

SPECIAL THANKS

H Heritage Malta

Produced by
Mizzi Design and Graphic Services Ltd

Printed in Malta at
Gutenberg Press Ltd

ISBN: 978-99932-7-406-3

CONTENTS

FOREWORD

I n 1942 an epic naval operation was mounted so as to relieve Malta from the onslaught of attacks by the forces of the Axis. This operation was codenamed "Pedestal"- or "*il-Convoy ta' Santa Marija*" as it is better known in Malta and Gozo.

MaltaPost is commemorating the 70th anniversary of this historical event with the issue of a unique set of no less than eighty-eight postage stamps. The set depicts vessels that took part in or contributed towards Operation Pedestal. Artist Cedric Galea Pirotta was commissioned to paint each of the eighty-eight vessels and the quality of his work truly befits the occasion.

The men taking part in Pedestal must have gone through hell. For example, the gallant tanker SS *Ohio* withstood persistent Stuka dive bomber attacks, had a Ju87 crash on her deck and when a Ju88 was brought down it bounced off the water and crashed into the vessel's side! Yet Ohio, after much effort by the Royal Navy, her captain and crew, and survivors from other ships, still made it to Grand Harbour!

Il-Convoy ta' Santa Marija is undoubtedly an iconic landmark event in the history of our country and it is therefore only fitting that those who paid the ultimate price in this operation be commemorated in a Roll of Honour which is reproduced in this book.

MaltaPost is proud of the fact that its stamps and other philatelic issues seek to commemorate the many events of note, customs, culture and history which together form our national identity. Considerable research has been undertaken to ensure historical accuracy and I thank all those who contributed towards this publication, which will complement the various others that preceded it.

I believe that John A Mizzi has brought together in one publication a number of related anecdotes and background accounts which may not have been widely known until now, thereby making this an important addition to the records of the fascinating history of Malta and Gozo.

Joseph Said
Chairman
MaltaPost

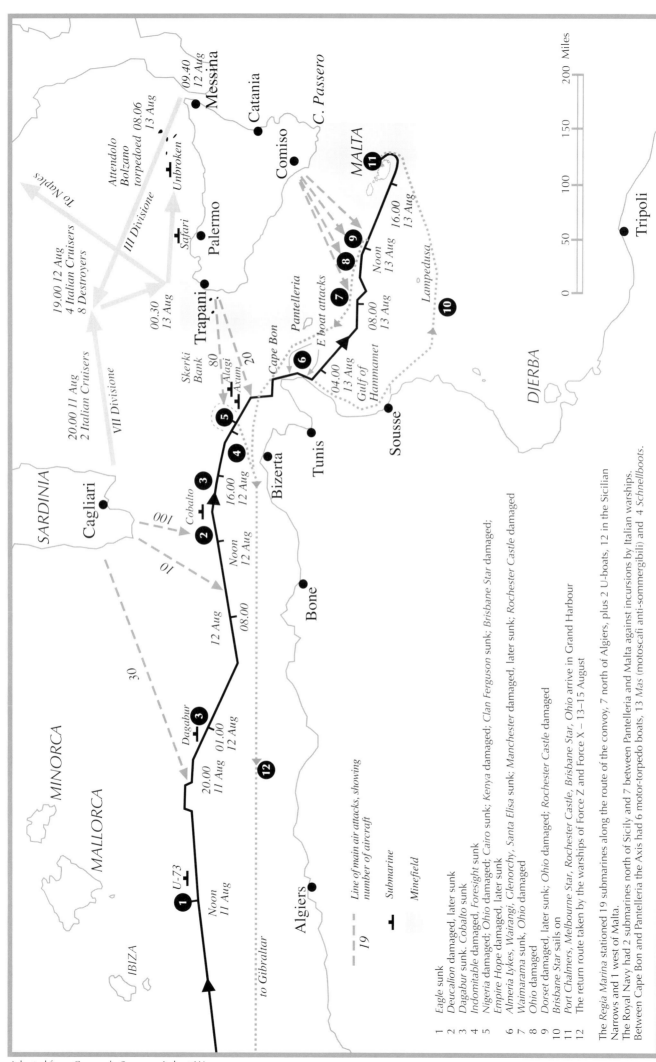

Adapted from *Comando Supremo*-Italy at War

OPERATION PEDESTAL

By the Spring of 1942 Malta had been under aerial siege for two years following Fascist Italy's entry in the war alongside Nazi Germany. The Luftwaffe had pulverized the island with incessant bombardment by wave after wave of bombers. The German Air Force controlled the air over the Mediterranean and the Royal Navy fought bitter battles to escort convoys to Malta from West and East, with heavy losses. In March a convoy of four ships was safely brought to near Malta despite the fierce opposition of the Axis air and sea forces, only for the ships to be sunk off the island and in harbour. By early July the island faced starvation and a target date was set for surrender if no supplies got through. The Italians were also carrying out extensive exercises for an invasion of the island.

A major attempt was made in June to get two large convoys to the embattled island as the loss of Malta would have spelt the end of this small island as the lynchpin of the war in the Mediterranean and the defence of Egypt and the Near and Middle East.

Convoy Harpoon sailed from the West with five merchant ships and a tanker and only two freighters reached the island, with the loss also of a number of escorting ships. Convoy Vigorous which sailed from Alexandria with eleven merchant ships was ordered to turn back after the loss of two of the ships and a number of escorts. The situation of Malta was now critical as never before and the British Prime Minister, Mr. Winston Churchill, was determined to pull all the stops and assemble the most powerful fleet for any single supply convoy operation of the war.

The plan was for Force Z, the main force, to take the merchant ships as far as the Sicilian Narrows, Force X up to the approaches to Malta, Force R to refuel the ships at sea, destroyers to sweep the mines for the convoy, to escort back to Gibraltar two ships that had reached Malta in June and to fly fighter aircraft to Malta.

The planning was developed at speed. The chosen commander, Vice-Admiral E. N. Syfret, who was at sea returning to the United Kingdom from the invasion of Madagascar in the Indian Ocean, was flown to Takoradi in West Africa and on to London on 13 July, and by 27 July he had drawn up the operation together with Rear-Admiral Harold Burrough and Rear-Admiral Arthur Lyster.

In all, thirteen modern freighters with a speed of no less than 15 knots were loaded with an even spread of commodities together with bombs and ammunition between decks, and on deck coal sacks and trucks filled with cans of kerosene, with tanker wagons on the side decks while imflammable cased petrol was carried as deck cargo; and chocolate, biscuits, wines, spirits, cigarettes and mails were packed in strong rooms and cargo lockers.

THE CONVOY WAS COMPOSED OF:

Almeria Lykes
(Captain W. Henderson),
Lykes Brothers, New Orleans,
8,000 grt.

Brisbane Star
(Captain R. Riley*)*,
Blue Star,
13,000 grt.

Clan Ferguson
(Captain A. Cossar*)*,
Clan Line,
7,347 grt.

Deucalion
(Captain R. Brown),
Blue Funnel Line,
8,000 grt.

Dorset
(Captain J. Tuckett),
Federal Steam Navigation Co.,
10,600 grt.

Empire Hope
(Captain G. Williams*)*,
Shaw, Saville and Albion,
12,688 grt.

Glenorchy
(Captain G. Leslie*)*,
Glen Line,
9,000 grt.

Melbourne Star
(Captain D.MacFarlane),
Blue Star,
12,806 grt.

Port Chalmers
(Captain H.G. Pinkney),
Port Line,
8,500 grt.

Rochester Castle
(Captain R. Wren),
Union Castle Line,
7,700 grt.

Santa Elisa
(Captain T. Thomson),
Grace Line, New York,
8,500 grt.

Waimarama
(Captain R. Pearce),
Shaw, Saville and Albion,
13,000 grt.

Wairangi
(Captain H. Gordon),
Shaw, Saville and Albion,
13,000 grt.

Ohio
(Captain D. Mason),
Texas Oil Co.,
10,000 grt.

Force Z aircraft carriers, seen from H.M.S. *Victorious*, H.M.S. *Indomitable* leading *Eagle*, with astern the cruiser H.M.S. *Charybdis*.

Most holds were filled with 4-gallon cans of petrol and kerosene, foodstuffs and flour. After loading at different ports the ships mustered in the estuary of the Clyde in Scotland.

Mr Churchill also requested the loan of the new American tanker *Ohio* from President Roosevelt as no British tanker fast enough was available, a request the president sanctioned despite the opposition of the U.S. Navy Department.

When the American tanker arrived at the Clyde in Scotland her master, Captain Peterson, was told to hand her over to Captain D. Mason of the *Eagle Oil Company* and a British crew. 11,500 tons of kerosene and diesel oil were loaded.

The commodore of the convoy, Commodore A.G. Venables, R.N. (Rtd.) joined *Port Chalmers*.

The North Russian convoys had been suspended in July after the disaster of Convoy P.Q.17 when 23 ships out of 24 which had sailed from Iceland to Arcangel were sunk. As a result the British Admiralty was able to draw heavily upon the warships of the Home Fleet. Other major units arrived from the Indian Ocean.

The forces engaged were:

Force Z - Battleships: **Nelson**, wearing the flag of Vice-Admiral E. N. Syfret; **Rodney.**

Carriers: **Victorious** (Rear-Admiral A.L. St. G. Lyster); **Indomitable** (Rear-Admiral D.W. Boyd); **Eagle; Furious.**

Destroyers: **Laforey; Lightning; Lookout; Quentin; Somali; Eskimo; Tartar; Ithuriel; Antelope; Wishart; Vansittart; Westcott; Wrestler; Zetland; Wilton.**

Force X - Cruisers: **Nigeria** (Rear-Admiral H.M. Burrough); **Kenya; Manchester; Cairo.**

Destroyers: **Ashanti; Intrepid; Icarus; Foresight; Fury; Pathfinder; Penn; Derwent; Bramham; Bicester; Ledbury.**

Escort for **Furious** (Operation Bellows)- Destroyers: **Keppel; Malcolm; Amazon; Venomous; Wolverine; Vidette.**

Force Y - Destroyers: **Badsworth; Matchless.**

Fleet oilers - **Brown Ranger; Dingledale; Abbeydale.**

Corvettes - **Jonquil; Geranium; Spirea; Coltsfoot; Burdoch; Armeiria.**

Malta Minesweepers - **Speedy; Rye; Hebe; Hythe.**

M.L.Flotilla - **121; 126; 134; 135; 168; 459; 462.**

Tugs - **Jaunty, Salvonia**

Submarines - **Safari; Unbroken; Uproar; Ultimatum; Unruffled; Utmost; United; Una, P 222.**

By the time the various ships were assembling in British waters, the island's defences were being further strengthened. *Eagle* had made a number of deliveries of Spitfires, in all 118, during four runs in June and July and *Furious* was ferrying another 37 to arrive on 11 August. The fighter defences of the island had gained some ascendancy following the air battles of mid-May.

The Regia Aeronautica by the end of July suspended its renewed offensive against the island. The fighter tactics introduced by the new Air Officer Commanding, Air Vice-Marshal Sir Keith Park, of meeting the enemy bombers before they reached the island, was giving results. In July the R.A.F. flew 1,800 sorties, lost 38 Spitfires, with half the pilots saved, and had claimed 137 enemy aircraft. The offensive by Wellingtons and Beauforts against enemy shipping supplying the Axis forces in Libya was resumed, while the Beaufighters carried the war to enemy airfields. More Beaufighters and Beauforts were flown to Malta from England and Egypt in anticipation of Operation Pedestal. To give air cover to the convoy from Malta there were 36 long-range Beaufighters and about 100 Spitfires.

British Intelligence at the time had a trump card, unknown to the Axis, which was revealed many years after the end of the war, and was, for some time, even kept from the Americans because earlier in the war secret information on Malta had been carelessly disclosed to the Germans. The enemy codes had been broken and operational messages were being intercepted to reveal the enemy plans.

The Axis were also concentrating their forces. As soon as the convoy was reported by their spies in the Straits of Gibraltar and by Vichy French aircraft, the German and Italian high commands started to position their submarines in the Western Mediterranean and to increase their fighter and bomber forces in Sardinia, Sicily and Pantelleria, in all some 650 Italian and 255 German aircraft. Units of the Regia Marina in the Thyrrenian Sea were put on the alert and E-boats positioned in the central Mediterranean, between Cape Bon and Pantelleria.

Sea Hurricanes

Victorious
809 Sqdn.	14 Fulmars
884 Sqdn.	6 Fulmars
885 Sqdn.	6 Sea Hurricanes
832 Sqdn.	12 Albacores

Indomitable
800 Sqdn.	12 Hurricanes
806 Sqdn.	10 Martlets
880 Sqdn.	10 Sea Hurricanes
827 Sqdn.	16 Albacores

Eagle
801 Sqdn.	16 Sea Hurricanes
813 Sqdn.	4 Sea Hurricanes

This was the strength on paper but severely reduced operationally by unserviceability. There was a further heavy loss when all but four of *Eagle's* Hurricanes went down with the ship, reducing the fighter strength by one-fourth. At the end of the day, before reversing course for Gibraltar on 12 August, *Victorious*, the only operational carrier could only assemble 10 Fulmars, 8 Sea Hurricanes and 3 Martlets – 7 Hurricanes had been shot down and four pilots killed; 7 Fulmars shot down, all two-man crews killed; and only three Martlets remained combat-worthy. The Fleet Air Arm claimed 39 Axis aircraft shot down.

Malta Operations
126 Sqdn.	Spitfires
185 Sqdn.	Spitfires
229 Sqdn.	Spitfires
249 Sqdn.	Spitfires
1435 Sqdn.	Spitfires
69 Sqdn.	Wellingtons/Baltimores
86 Sqdn.	Beauforts
89 Sqdn.	Beaufighters
159 Sqdn.	Liberators
248 Sqdn.	Beaufighters
252 Sqdn.	Beaufighters

Malta's fighters flew 414 sorties in defence of the convoy, 389 by Spitfires, including 97 long range, and 25 by Beaufighters. 14 enemy aircraft were claimed shot down for the loss of four Spitfires and one Beaufighter.

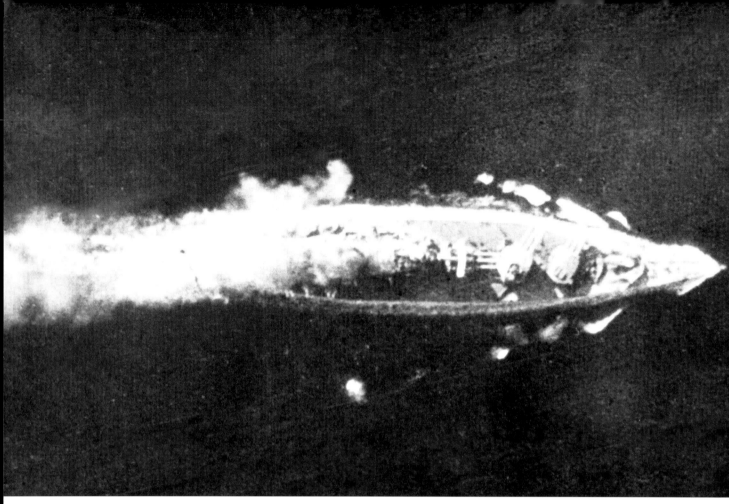

The battleship H.M.S. *Rodney* photographed by an enemy reconnaissance aircraft

The ships sailed on 2 August and various exercises were held during the passage to Gibraltar. Pedestal passed through the Straits in dense fog during the night of 9/10 August.

At the other end of the Mediterranean a bogus British convoy of four freighters escorted by four cruisers and 15 destroyers headed westwards from Haifa

Force Y – The destroyers H.M.S. *Badsworth* (above, left) and H.M.S. *Matchless* (above. right) escorted the merchant ships *Orari* (below, left) and *Troilus* (below, right) safely from Malta to Gibraltar

CONVOY DISPOSITIONS BETWEEN 10 AUGUST AND 6.00 AM 11 AUGUST

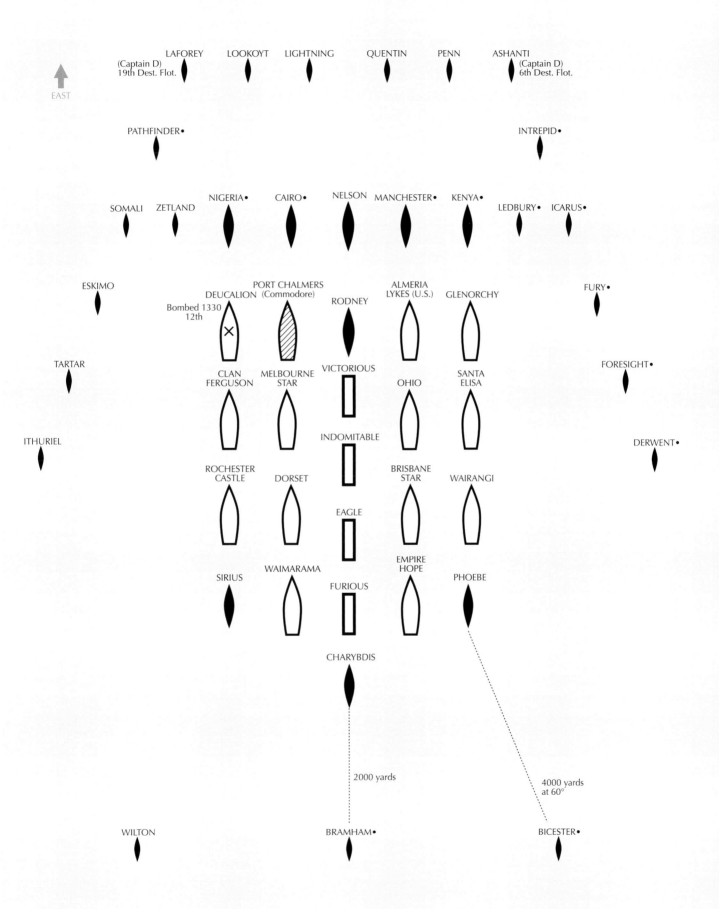

The convoy dispositions in the early stages of the operation between late on 10 August and the morning of 11 August, steaming at 13 ½ knots. The carriers changed station to fly off and recover their aircraft.
Warships marked • were to escort the freighters all the way to Malta. The warships of Force Z were to return to Gibraltar after escorting the merchant ships to as far as the approaches to the Sicilian Channel.

H.M.S. *Rodney* engages the enemy aircraft

and Port Said to try and deceive the Italian warships at Navarino and the Luftwaffe in Crete, which it did not, and the ships put into Alexandria on 11 August. Meanwhile the two ships which had reached Malta in the June convoy, *Troilus* and *Orari*, sailed westwards from Grand Harbour at night escorted by *Badsworth* and *Matchless* and, hugging the North African coast, escaped to arrive at Gibraltar on 14 August.

Italian SM 79 torpedo bombers attacking the convoy

TUESDAY, 11 AUGUST

When the convoy was some 580 miles west of Malta, soon after noon on 11 August, *Furious* started to launch her Spitfires for their flight to Malta but the operation was interrupted dramatically when *U-73* penetrated the destroyer screen and hit *Eagle* with four torpedoes; the carrier sank in eight minutes, with the loss of 160 of her company of 1,160 and all of her aircraft bar four, nearly one fourth of the convoy's fighter strength.

THE END OF H.M.S. EAGLE

Empire Hope steams past the sinking *Eagle*.

H.M.S. *Eagle* sank in eight minutes after being hit by four torpedoes fired by *U-73*, whose captain was Kapitän Leutenant Helmut Rosenbaum (inset).

Survivors of *Eagle* are rescued by boats from the destroyer H.M.S. *Lookout*. Nearly 1,000 were saved, 160 lost (below).

Sea Hurricanes ranged for take-off from the deck of H.M.S. *Victorious*.

Furious having flown off her Spitfires was joined by her destroyers to return to Gibraltar; on the way one of her escorts, *Wolverine*, during the night ran down the Italian submarine *Dagabur* which sank with all hands.

The first bombing attack on the convoy was made a quarter of an hour after sunset on 11 August by 27 Ju88s from Sicily and three He111 torpedo bombers, a number of which were shot down; there was no damage to the ships. The oilers had by then refueled three cruisers and 26 destroyers.

Acting on information from intercepted enemy signals, quickly decrypted, eleven Beaufighters from Malta attacked the airfields in southern Sardinia and destroyed five SM 79 torpedo bombers and damaged a very large number of others, with no loss to themselves. On their return flight they were reported to have seen two Italian cruisers and two destroyers sailing eastwards from Cagliari, after an earlier report by a Wellington on patrol of another four cruisers and eight destroyers sailing westwards. In fact these R.A.F. aircraft had been sent to confirm enemy naval movements revealed by *Ultra* to Malta command headquarters.

WEDNESDAY, 12 AUGUST

The first attack on 12 August came at 8.30 a.m. by 30 Ju88s which were intercepted

A Martlet takes off from the flight deck of H.M.S. *Indomitable*

CONVOY DISPOSITIONS BETWEEN 6 AM 11 AUGUST – 6.30 PM 12 AUGUST

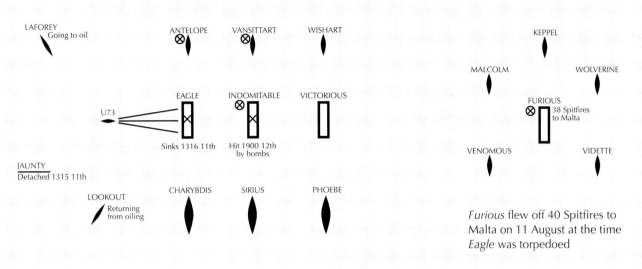

LAFOREY
Going to oil

ANTELOPE

VANSITTART

WISHART

KEPPEL

MALCOLM

WOLVERINE

EAGLE

INDOMITABLE

VICTORIOUS

FURIOUS
38 Spitfires
to Malta

U73

Sinks 1316 11th

Hit 1900 12th
by bombs

VENOMOUS

VIDETTE

JAUNTY
Detached 1315 11th

LOOKOUT
Returning
from oiling

CHARYBDIS

SIRIUS

PHOEBE

Furious flew off 40 Spitfires to
Malta on 11 August at the time
Eagle was torpedoed

H.M.S. *Eagle* is torpedoed by *U-73* and sinks in eight
minutes at 1.16 p.m. on 11 August

EAST

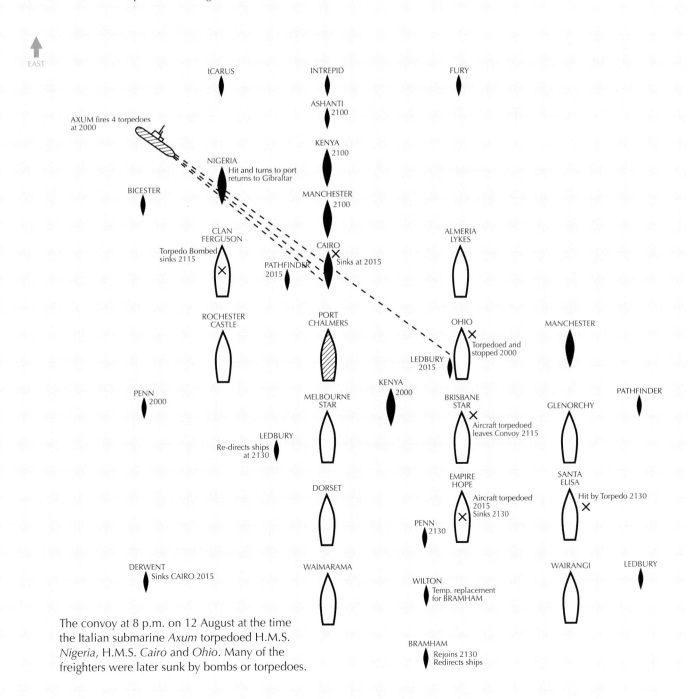

ICARUS

INTREPID

FURY

ASHANTI
2100

AXUM fires 4 torpedoes
at 2000

KENYA
2100

NIGERIA
Hit and turns to port
returns to Gibraltar

BICESTER

MANCHESTER
2100

CLAN
FERGUSON
Torpedo Bombed
sinks 2115

ALMERIA
LYKES

CAIRO
Sinks at 2015

PATHFINDER
2015

ROCHESTER
CASTLE

PORT
CHALMERS

OHIO
Torpedoed and
stopped 2000

MANCHESTER

LEDBURY
2015

PENN
2000

KENYA
2000

PATHFINDER

MELBOURNE
STAR

BRISBANE
STAR
Aircraft torpedoed
leaves Convoy 2115

GLENORCHY

LEDBURY
Re-directs ships
at 2130

DORSET

EMPIRE
HOPE
Aircraft torpedoed
2015
Sinks 2130

SANTA
ELISA
Hit by Torpedo 2130

PENN
2130

DERWENT
Sinks CAIRO 2015

WAIMARAMA

WAIRANGI

LEDBURY

WILTON
Temp. replacement
for BRAMHAM

The convoy at 8 p.m. on 12 August at the time
the Italian submarine *Axum* torpedoed H.M.S.
Nigeria, H.M.S. *Cairo* and *Ohio*. Many of the
freighters were later sunk by bombs or torpedoes.

BRAMHAM
Rejoins 2130
Redirects ships

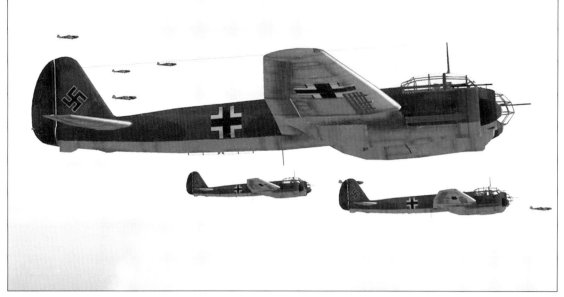

Ju88s in formation

An He111 launches a torpedo

by the defending naval fighters, in all on paper, 48 Sea Hurricanes,10 Martlets and 16 Fulmars. The carriers also had 28 Albacores.

During the early morning the Italians lost five aircraft and a further two were shot down in error by the Cagliari defences. Undismayed, the Regia Aeronautica amassed its squadrons and dispatched them in relays against the convoy

- 12 high altitude bombers, 80 dive-bombers, 6 low-level bombers, 42 torpedo bombers, 45 fighters and an assortment of other types, including a radio-controlled SM 79 packed with 1000 kg of explosives which failed to respond to signals and crashed in the mountains south of Constantine in Algeria. The attacking aircraft failed to make any hits, although one bomb struck the flight-deck of *Victorious* but failed to explode. 37 Ju88s from Sicily attacked in between the Regia Aeronautica forays and one unexploded bomb pierced the deck of the freighter *Deucalion* and two others burst in the sea alongside her and she was stopped. Some of the crew lowered lifeboats and pulled away but were ordered back. With her speed reduced and down by the head, her captain was instructed to proceed independently, hugging the coast with *Bramham* as escort.

SM 79 torpedo bombers

H.M.S. *Ithuriel* races at high speed to ram and sink the Italian submarine *Cobalto* which had surfaced after being depth charged

Ithuriel rams *Cobalto* abaft the conning tower
The crew leave the sinking submarine. Three officers and 38 ratings were picked up by the destroyer

THE VARIOUS FREIGHTERS ABLAZE
PHOTOGRAPHED BY AXIS AIRCRAFT

Indomitable was put out of action. Seven officers and 42 men were killed

The two lifts of *Indomitable* were damaged, and 20 feet of the flight deck ripped, with a large section of the hangar deck shattered and several of the Albacore pilots killed

Indomitable under attack by Luftwaffe Ju87s is obscured by smoke and splashes

Pedestal thereupon steamed north of Galite Island, off Tunisia, evading a number of attacks by enemy submarines. *Ithuriel* rammed and sank *Cobalto*, rescuing 41 Italian sailors.

The convoy was now approaching the Skerki Bank when at 7.30 p.m. a large formation of German Ju87s, Italian SM79 torpedo bombers and scores of fighters was intercepted by the Sea Hurricanes from *Victorious*. *Indomitable*'s flight deck was hit by three bombs from a German Ju87 and the carrier was rendered useless as a fighting unit. The destroyer *Foresight* was torpedoed by an SM 79 and her stern blown away. *Indomitable*'s aircraft were ordered to land on *Victorious* and the damaged carrier, now a liability, was next morning ordered to return to Gibraltar, together with *Rodney* which had developed boiler defects and *Ithuriel* with damaged bows in ramming *Cobalto*; they were escorted by a screen of six destroyers.

Fires burn on the flight deck of the carrier *Indomitable* after she was hit

H.M.S. *Foresight* was struck by an aerial torpedo dropped by an SM 79 and her back broken. She sank in a few hours when it proved impossible to tow her to Gibraltar and H.M.S. *Tartar* torpedoed her

Force Z parted company from the convoy at about 7 p.m., as had been previously planned, to return to Gibraltar. The heavy units could not be risked in the Sicilian Narrows and the battleships, carriers and 11 destroyers were withdrawn and 4 cruisers and 12 destroyers were left to guard the convoy at the time the Italian submarines were taking up station in the northern approaches to the channel. Flotillas of Italian torpedo-boats, together with German e-boats, reinforced by others from Crete, were positioning between Sicily and Tunisia.

The Italian submarine *Axum* sighted the convoy 30 miles north-west of Cape Bon at 8 p.m. and launched four torpedoes, all of which hit. *Nigeria*, struck below the bridge, started to settle by the bows. Fifty were killed. Admiral Burrough, now in tactical command,

transferred his flag to the destroyer *Ashanti* and sent his flagship to Gibraltar. Hit at the same time by two torpedoes was the cruiser *Cairo* whose crew were taken off and she was sunk by H.M.S. *Pathfinder*. Twenty-two were killed. Also hit was *Ohio*. She had a hole 24 feet by 27 feet amidships aft of the bridge, caught fire and stopped. When motion was resumed she could only manoeuvre slowly in circles.

Next to go was *Empire Hope*, with a 15-foot torpedo hole in her side and two direct bomb hits. She became a tower of flames although all her crew managed to escape. She was torpedoed and sunk by H.M.S. *Penn*.

Now came the turn of *Brisbane Star* which was hit in the bow by a torpedo from an He111. Her master, Captain Riley, realising he could not keep pace with the remnants of

The Italian submarine *Axum*

The cruiser *Nigeria*, flagship of Rear-Admiral Burrough, down by the bow after being hit by a torpedo fired by *Axum*. She listed to port and the admiral and his staff transferred to the destroyer *Ashanti*. *Nigeria* was sent back to Gibraltar. Four officers and 48 ratings were killed.

Admiral Burrough on the bridge of *Ashanti* after transferring from *Nigeria*.

Captain Richard Onslow, Captain (D) 6th Destroyer Flotilla, on the bridge of *Ashanti*.

Sub Lieut. Terence Lewin, a gunnery officer on *Ashanti*. He retired from the Navy in 1979 as Admiral of the Fleet.

the convoy, left the formation and headed south intending to hug the Tunisian coast and proceed independently to Malta.

Next, *Clan Ferguson* carrying ammunition was hit by an aerial torpedo and she blew up. A lifeboat with 40 crewmen reached Zembra Island next morning and the men were interned by the Vichy French; other survivors on rafts were picked up by the Italian submarine *Bronzo* and by Italian and German

rescue aircraft and seacraft. Shortly after 9 p.m. the Italian submarine *Alagi* torpedoed the cruiser *Kenya*, seriously damaging her bow.

The convoy was by now disrupted and the Commodore, Commander Venables, in *Port Chalmers*, reversed course and signaled *Melbourne Star* and *Dorset* to follow suit, followed by *Almeria Lykes*. The masters of the two British ships decided to disregard Venables' orders to return to Gibraltar and resumed course for Malta. *Ledbury* went up to the American freighter whereupon her captain also turned back on an east-south-east course. *Bramham* met with *Port Chalmers* soon after midnight near Cani Rocks and the freighter reversed course eastward to be joined by *Penn* across the minefield off Cape Bon.

The enemy E-boats were waiting in ambush in the narrow waters between the Tunisian coast and Pantelleria.

The convoy rounded Cape Bon shortly before midnight with the leading warships following the minesweeping destroyers and accompanied by *Glenorchy*, *Almeria Lykes* and *Wairangi*. Strung out behind them were

Ohio is hit by a torpedo fired by *Axum* which opened a hole, 24 feet by 27 feet.

A bomb explodes alongside *Clan Ferguson*

Melbourne Star, *Waimarama*, *Santa Elisa*, *Rochester Castle* and *Dorset,* escorted only by *Pathfinder*. Further astern *Ledbury* was escorting *Ohio* and further behind *Penn* was accompanying *Port Chalmers*. *Brisbane Star* was on her own close to the Tunisian coast. The ships had covered over 800 miles from Gibraltar with some 300 miles to reach Malta.

Soon after midnight the warships in the van picked up signs of prowling small craft on their radar screens. The Italian *MAS* darted at the ships in the dark and fired their torpedoes from close range. The torpedoes missed. The German E-boats joined in. The beacon lights at Cape Bon and at Keliba were powerful enough to illuminate the ships and the speeding craft picked *Manchester*, the only undamaged cruiser, and fired their torpedoes at point-blank range and hit her starboard side. The engine and boiler rooms were flooded and the ship stopped. The freighters following *Manchester* took evasive action to avoid collision.

H.M.S. *Kenya* under heavy attack

Kenya was badly damaged by a torpedo from the Italian submarine *Alagi,* but despite the extensive damage to her bow, the cruiser continued to keep speed with the convoy

Despite strenuous efforts to get the cruiser moving, she remained immobile. *Pathfinder* drew up alongside and took off 163 of the crew and the rest took to their Carley floats and boats. The ship was scuttled and she sank in 20 fathoms at 5.50 a.m. Later *Eskimo* and *Somali* rescued 13 officers and 308 ratings from rafts. Captain Drew, 38 officers and 487 ratings reached the shore and were interned by the Vichy French in Algeria. They were released during the Anglo-American landings in North Africa in November 1942. Later Captain Drew and several of the ship's officers were court-martialed and the court ruled the cruiser had been scuttled prematurely, a decision disputed by many, especially the crew.

Manchester is attacked by two Italian E-boats during the night which fired torpedoes hitting her starboard side, which immobilsed her, The crew abandoned the cruiser which was scuttled

A German *schnellboot*

Survivors of H.M.S. *Manchester*

The Italian *MAS* E-boat

Ledbury closes in on *Ohio* to attempt a tow of the tanker

The progress of the convoy was being monitored with mounting concern at the operations rooms of Malta Command at Lascaris as aircraft from Malta kept a watch on the movements of the Italian naval squadron in the Thyrrenian Sea which was steaming south-west. An attack on the merchant ships by surface ships would have meant their total annihilation. The Italian battleships could not leave Taranto because of shortage of fuel but the reunion of the naval units from Spezia, Cagliari. Naples and Messina had been observed, after a tip-off by *Ultra,* some 35 miles west-north-west of the island of Ustica steaming south. The Regia Marina planned to meet the convoy early the next morning south of Pantelleria.

The naval squadron comprised the cruisers *Gorizia, Trieste, Bolzano, Eugenio di Savoia, Montecuccoli, Attendolo* and 11 destroyers. The R.A.F. from Malta kept up its bluff of strength by illuminating the ships at intervals and sending plain messages to give the impression that a large striking force was on its way. Behind the scenes Supermarina was alarmed and requested air cover from

H.M.S. *Penn* alongside the starboard side of *Ohio* in an attempt to tow her the final leg to Malta on the morning of 14 August as the destroyer played martial music

the Luftwaffe. This was refused. An appeal was made to Mussolini to intervene with Hitler, who sided with his commanders. At 1. 56 a.m. on 13 August the shadowing R.A.F. aircraft reported the force had turned north-east when north of Trapani, confirming an *Ultra* decrypt, and appeared to be heading in the direction of Palermo. Mussolini had cancelled the operation and thereby spared the convoy.

The Royal Navy submarine *Unbroken* from Malta was waiting for the returning warships and she torpedoed *Bolzano* and *Attendolo* some 12 miles west-south-west of Stromboli, both cruisers being put out of service for the rest of the war.

War Headquarters, inside Lascaris Bastions

The E-boats continued to pick off the ships which were dispersed off the Tunisian coast during the night.

Glenorchy was hit by two torpedoes at 2 a.m. and the engine-room was flooded. The order was given to abandon ship and her crew of 124 left in boats but her master, Captain George Leslie, refused to leave and went down with her. The men were interned by the Vichy French at Sfax from where they were released following the Anglo-American landings in November. The Italian E-boats picked up nine men from a raft. Eight men were lost.

Wairangi was torpedoed from 500 yards away by another *MAS* at 3.10 a.m. The pumps could not cope with the influx of water in the engine room and holds and the captain decided to abandon ship. The crew took to the boats and

The Italian cruiser *Attendolo*, minus her bow section after being torpedoed by H.M.S. *Unbroken*

The cruiser *Bolzano* is stopped after being torpedoed by H.M.S *Unbroken,* with most of her crew on the forecastle while attempts are made to control a fire amidships

rafts and were later picked up by *Eskimo*. She remained afloat for some time and was attacked by He111s with torpedoes, all of which missed. The water-logged freighter sank later in the morning.

The two American ships were also disposed of by the German and Italian E-boats. *Santa Elisa* was hit by a torpedo from point-blank range in her starboard bow

The crew of the submarine *Unbroken* cheer their Captain, Lieut. Cdr. Alastair Mars

Dorset under attack. She was severely damaged by near misses to the extent that it was impossible to fight the fire in her No. 4 hold. Her crew transferred to H.M.S. *Bramham* and efforts to tow her failed. She eventually sank

and her cargo of aviation spirit ignited. Fire engulfed the ship with a loud explosion. The crew pulled away in three lifeboats and were rescued by *Penn*.

The end of *Almeria Lykes* was a different story. She was hit in the bulkhead of No.1 hold at the same time at *Wairangi*. Her master, Captain Wheeler Henderson, 59, had been born in London but had become an American citizen and was resident in Galveston, Texas; he realized he could continue to steer his ship to Malta. His unruly American crew of 72 thought otherwise. Only three of them were under 26, were anti-British and resented being in the convoy to Malta, which they had never heard of before. They had been complaining at not getting four eggs for breakfast and not enough food, oblivous this was a mission to an island facing starvation. Wheeler ordered abandon ship conscious the crew would do so anyway. When *Pathfinder* arrived her captain refused to pick them up as he thought they should return to the ship. They refused and the captain returned to the ship with four others, including the British liaison officer, Lieut. Cdr. H.S. Marshall, to place charges and scuttle *Almeria Lykes* to prevent her falling into enemy hands. She was still afloat at 9.30 a.m. when *Somali* turned up and picked up the American seamen and took

A torpedo launched at *Port Chalmers* by an SM79 is caught in the ship's starboard paravane. She stopped and then went astern in an attempt to release it. The gear was slipped and the torpedo exploded in some 400 fathoms jarring the ship.

them to Gibraltar. Marshall in his report to Admiral Syfret wrote: "the abandonment of this ship is one of shame."

CONVOY DISPOSITIONS BETWEEN MIDNIGHT – 6.25PM 13 AUGUST

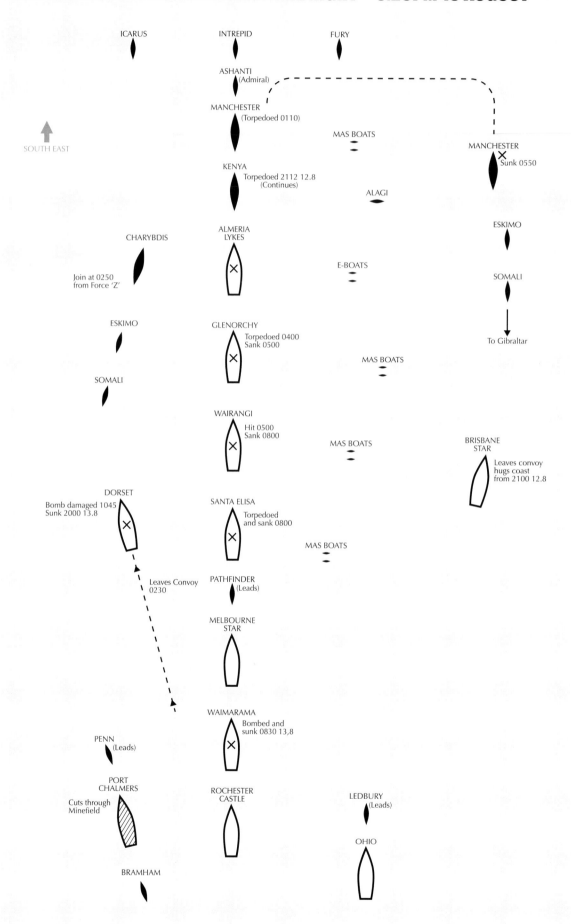

ICARUS

INTREPID

FURY

ASHANTI
(Admiral)

MANCHESTER
(Torpedoed 0110)

MAS BOATS

MANCHESTER
✕ Sunk 0550

SOUTH EAST

KENYA
Torpedoed 2112 12.8
(Continues)

ALAGI

ESKIMO

CHARYBDIS

ALMERIA
LYKES

E-BOATS

SOMALI

Join at 0250
from Force 'Z'

To Gibraltar

ESKIMO

GLENORCHY
Torpedoed 0400
Sank 0500

MAS BOATS

SOMALI

WAIRANGI
Hit 0500
Sank 0800

MAS BOATS

BRISBANE
STAR
Leaves convoy
hugs coast
from 2100 12.8

DORSET
Bomb damaged 1045
Sunk 2000 13.8

SANTA ELISA
Torpedoed
and sank 0800

MAS BOATS

Leaves Convoy
0230

PATHFINDER
(Leads)

MELBOURNE
STAR

WAIMARAMA
Bombed and
sunk 0830 13,8

PENN
(Leads)

PORT
CHALMERS
Cuts through
Minefield

ROCHESTER
CASTLE

LEDBURY
(Leads)

OHIO

BRAMHAM

The ships in convoy are massacred by *MAS* and E-boats during the night of 12-13 August
H.M.S. *Manchester* is torpedoed and sunk by her captain off the Tunisian coast.
Brisbane Star escapes hugging the Tunisian coast.

An *SM79* torpedo bomber flying at mast-top height over one of the escorting warships

With the E-boats withdrawn, the surviving ships reassembled. These were *Melbourne Star*, *Waimarama*, *Rochester Castle*, *Dorset*, *Port Chalmers* with *Ohio* straggling behind astern and *Brisbane Star* on her own steaming slowly down the east coast of Tunisia, pursued both by the Vichy French authorities and a submarine, with Captain Riley resisting the crew's insistence to scuttle the ship so they could go safely ashore.

Although now approaching Malta and expecting air cover the ships were without any fighter-directing ships after the loss of *Cairo* and the withdrawal of *Nigeria*. It was to be a day of persistent enemy air attacks

H.M.S. *Ledury*

with the loss of *Dorset* and the horrendous end of *Waimarama*.

THURSDAY, 13 AUGUST

The Luftwaffe continued with their attacks in the early hours of 13 August and at 8.10 a.m. twelve Ju88s from Catania found four ships 30 miles south-east of Pantelleria - *Rochester Castle* leading *Waimarama*, *Melbourne Star* and *Ohio*. Three Junkers made for *Waimarama* and one of these gained four hits on her. The deck cargo of high octane fuel and ammunition blew up with a shattering roar and a ball of fire. The ship disintegrated and disappeared in a flash. The sea caught fire and a gigantic column of black smoke darkened the sky. *Melbourne Star* steamed through the burning sea, her paint was scorched and her lifeboats set on fire. 36 of her crew leapt over the side expecting their ship to blow up. *Ohio* turned quickly to port barely avoiding the flames. With *Waimarama* went her master, Captain R.S. Pearce and 86 of her complement of 107.

Lieut. Cdr. Roger Hill in *Ledbury* ignored Admiral Burrough's instructions not to go too near the burning sea and took the destroyer to the heart of the furnace to rescue the screaming men. While some climbed up ropes and scrambling nets let down the destroyer's side, others were plucked from

Volunteers on *Ohio* attempt to rig a tow-line

Ohio off Grand Harbour is kept afloat by the destroyers *Bramham,* on her port side, and *Penn*

the conflagration by the ship's boats and by individual sailors who jumped over the side. Some 20 men in all were rescued as were the 26 who had abandoned *Melbourne Star.*

The Axis aircraft continued to attack in wave after wave to be met by the fighters operating from Malta at extreme range. Several were shot down by the ships' anti-aircraft guns as was one of the R.A.F Spitfires from Malta, the Australian pilot, Flight Sgt. Robert Buntine, being killed

Ohio was near-missed by a 500-lb bomb which caused further damage to her battered hull. One Italian Stuka was shot down and smashed into the tanker's side, landing on the poop. Shortly after, a Ju88 hit the water some 50 feet from *Ohio* and bounced onto the foredeck, blowing out the boiler fires and stopping the tanker dead.

Dorset had been attacked by Stukas when a heavy bomb penetrated one of her holds, flooding the engines and starting a fire close

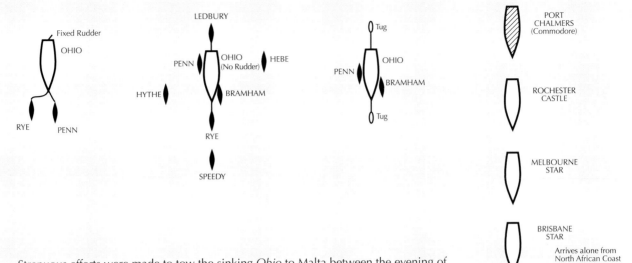

Strenuous efforts were made to tow the sinking *Ohio* to Malta between the evening of 13 August until the morning of 15 August. The three merchant ships, *Port Chalmers*, *Rochester Castle* and *Melbourne Star,* which arrived in the evening of 13 August were joined by *Brisbane Star* at noon on 14 August.

to the high octane. The order was given to abandon ship and she was left ablaze and still afloat. All her crew were rescued by *Bramham*. The Luftwafe targeted the burning ship in successive attacks and she finally sank at 7 p.m.

Rochester Castle, which had been damaged earlier by near misses, was at 10 a.m. hit by three bombs which lifted the ship out of the water and dislocated the engine. Fire spread but was got under control and the ship's engines were restarted. The air attacks continued and at one stage, at 2.45 p.m., the Ju88s bombed the Italian submarines *Alagi* and *Dessie* by mistake, injuring the captain of *Dessie* and eight of the crew.

By 4 p.m. air cover for the convoy was being provided by the short-range Spitfires and the Malta Escort Force had made contact. The ordeal for *Port Chalmers*, *Rochester Castle* and *Melbourne Star* seemed over with Grand Harbour now in distant view.

Brisbane Star was still proceeding on her own having steamed through the Tunisian territorial waters, with Captain Riley bluffing his way with the Vichy French authorities who insisted he anchors when he was crossing the Gulf of Hammamet. He also had problems with the crew after a

periscope was seen following his ship and the men feared that as soon as they reached international waters they would be torpedoed. They became almost mutinous, demanding the ship be scuttled before she was torpedoed. He ordered them all to assemble on deck and they were given an ultimatum by the naval liaison officer, Lieut. E.D. Symes: "If you do not obey orders the naval and military personnel at my orders would turn their guns on you." They obeyed.

At 5 p.m. on 12 August a small French craft chased the ship and Captain Riley had to stop. *Brisbane Star* was boarded by two French

Port Chalmers berths in Grand Harbour

Rochester Castle

THE SURVIVING SHIPS ARE WELCOMED BY CHEERING CROWDS

Melbourne Star

Port Chalmers

Brisbane Star

The sinking *Ohio* with *Bramham* lashed to her port side and assisted by tugs is moved slowly to Parlatorio Wharf

officers who ordered him to follow them inshore for the ship to be interned. But Captain Riley invited them to drinks in his cabin and persuaded them to let him proceed. When they left they also took with them one of the injured hands, a greaser who died. Riley made for Malta during the night, steering south-east, and by morning was being given air cover by Beaufighters from Malta when south of Linosa. The freighter was attacked by Italian bombers later in the day but was unscathed and continued steaming towards Malta.

Strenuous efforts were being made to get *Ohio* to Malta before she sank. Her engines were out of action. *Penn* secured a towline to the tanker which was drawing 37 feet. The 30,000 tons deadweight of the hulk proved too much as she contracted the tow by veering steadily to port and the line parted. The attacks continued and the tanker was abandoned. The crew returned to *Penn* at 2.15 p.m.

The R.A.F. kept a protective screen over *Ohio* as the German and Italian aircraft continued with their attacks. The minesweeper *Rye* and *ML 121* and *ML 161* arrived later in the afternoon when the tanker's exhausted crew volunteered to return to the ship with a naval party at 5.45 p.m. to make another attempt to tow her.

At that moment three of the surviving merchant ships were approaching Valletta through the swept channel off Delimara and at 6.30 p.m. *Rochester Castle* led *Port Chalmers* and *Melbourne Star* into Grand Harbour to a hero's welcome. The imminent arrival of a convoy was general knowledge on the island, not only because of the Italian radio broadcasts but also by the preparations being made to receive the ships. All the vantage points overlooking Grand Harbour were packed solid with people cheering and waving flags, with the band of the Royal Malta Artillery on St.

Elmo bastion playing *Rule Britannia* and other rousing music.

The rudder of *Ohio* was partly repaired and the tanker was pulled forward but she kept veering to port. The tow was again stopped when at 7.10 p.m. *Ohio* was attacked by eight Ju88s and one bomb penetrated the boat deck and exploded in the engine room. *ML 168* was badly damaged and was sent back to Malta. *Ohio* appeared to be sinking and the crew told to abandon her. Most of the crew rejoined *Penn* and the rest were picked up by *ML 121*.

At dusk two more attacks further damaged *Ohio*'s structure. At this stage, *Bramham* joined the group after rescuing the crew of *Dorset* which finally sank at 8 p.m. A further effort was made to tow *Ohio* just before midnight when not far from Malta; this also failed. There was a short break for rest.

FRIDAY, 14 AUGUST

At daybreak on 14 August the enemy aircraft resumed their attacks on the tanker which lasted all day. With the arrival of *Ledbury*, packed with survivors from the sunken ships, it was decided to board *Ohio* again and many of the survivors and the tanker's crew volunteered to man her guns and clear wreckage. Soon after, at 11 a.m., the minesweeper *Speedy* arrived with Commander H.J.A.S. Jerome of the Malta Escort Force. The Italian Stukas attacked and dropped oil bombs and further towing attempts were interrupted by the bombers with near misses.

Commander Jerome took over from Admiral Burrough the responsibility for the convoy. An attempt was made to move the tanker with *Bramham* and *Penn* alongside, one on each side, with *Rye* towing from ahead, proceeding at six knots as *Penn* played music on her PA system. Air was pumped into the oil tanks by an air compressor to assist her buoyancy as the tanker was sinking six inches every hour. The R.A.F. maintained an umbrella over the ships but the Ju87s succeeded to penetrate and drop a 1,000 lb.

Unloading the cargo from *Melbourne Star*

bomb astern of the tanker, twisting her screws and holing her stern. *Ohio* continued to move ahead at five knots and by late afternoon the tanker was being coaxed with difficulty through the swept channel off Delimara where the Assistant King's Harbour Master, Cdr. J. P. Pilditch, in *Robust* took over. The tug in attempting to assist the tow smashed hard into the side of *Penn* and was sent back to Malta while the destroyers resumed the tow. It was now very dark and *Ohio* was being guided with difficulty through the swept channel off Delimara at 2 a.m. The searchlights from shore lit up the scene when there were reports of surface craft and a submarine in the area and the guns of Fort Bingemma, Fort Madliena and Fort Leonardo opened up. This infuriated the *Ohio* group for being exposed to possible enemy attacks. The guns were silenced.

SATURDAY, 15 AUGUST

On 15 August, feast day of Santa Marija, Cdr. Pilditch, and a pilot, Lawrence Attard, boarded *Ohio* at 6.45 a.m. and the tanker, her decks almost awash, passed through the breakwater arms at 8 a.m. She was shepherded by *Bramham* and *Penn* and tugs to hold her from sinking. She was manoeuvred alongside the sunken hulk of the auxiliary tanker *Plumleaf* at Parlatorio Wharf in French Creek and her fuel oil immediately discharged into the local tanker *Boxall*. *Ohio* appeared to be breaking her back and as her tanks were emptied they were flooded with sea water to ballast the slowly sinking tanker, which eventually settled gently on the seabed.

Lieut. Cdr. Hill wrote several years later: "The great ramparts and battlements of Malta, built against the earlier siege by the Turks, were lined and black with people. Thousands and thousands of cheering people were on the ramparts, on the foreshore, on the rooftops, the roads, paths and at every window. Everywhere bands were playing; bands of all the Services and Maltese bands. The uneven thumps of the drums and crash of the cymbals were echoed back from the great walls. The sense of achievement; the relief of having brought *Ohio* there after so much striving; to have no casualties amongst my own people, and perhaps above all, the knowledge that the ship would be secured and I could sleep and sleep – these were some of the emotions sweeping over me as I stood on the bridge, berthing the ship bow and stern in French Creek... the *Ohio* being pushed to the wharf to discharge her oil was the most wonderful moment of my life."

Churchill sent a signal to *Penn*, *Bramham* and *Ledbury*: "Well done!" The Prime Minister was in Moscow for his first meeting with the Soviet leader, Joseph Stalin, to inform him of the plans for Operation Torch, the Anglo-U.S. landings in French North Africa scheduled for November.

In Cairo before flying to Moscow on 10 August, Churchill had relieved General Sir Claude Auchinleck, the Commander-in-Chief, Middle East, who had refused to launch an operation in the Western Desert before mid-September which Churchill was pressing for to ease the pressure on Malta, vital for future operations in the Mediterranean.

The prime minister had given instructions to the Admiralty to keep him informed of the progress of Pedestal and when told of the arrival of five ships and of the heavy losses sustained, he asked that a message be sent to the naval commanders and all those involved "in the crash through of supplies to Malta which cannot fail to have an important influence on the immediate future of the war in the Mediterranean." He remarked that the effort was worth the cost.

His thoughts were further revealed in his speech in the House of Commons on 8 September: "… this price, though heavy, was not excessive for the result obtained for Malta is not only as bright a gem as shines in the King's crown, but its effective action against the enemy's communications with Libya and Egypt is essential to the whole strategic position in the Middle East."

Plans were made in earnest to assemble as many as 32 ships with 170,000 tons of supplies for convoy to Malta from both Gibraltar and Alexandria as the 33,000 tons which were unloaded, it was estimated, would last for about a month.

Injured members of the crew are taken ashore on arrival in Grand Harbour

The survivors of *Waimarama* are helped down the rope ladder alongside H.M.S. *Ledbury*

ARTEFACTS FROM OPERATION PEDESTAL ON DISPLAY AT THE NATIONAL WAR MUSEUM IN VALLETTA

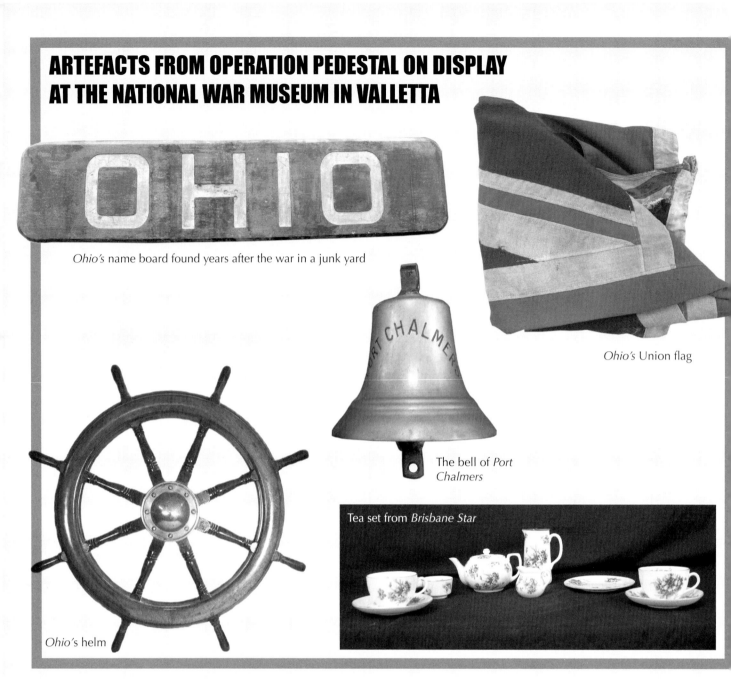

Ohio's name board found years after the war in a junk yard

Ohio's Union flag

The bell of *Port Chalmers*

Tea set from *Brisbane Star*

Ohio's helm

There was some concern when the German commander of the Afrika Korps, Field Marshal Erwin Rommel, launched an attack on 2 September to advance into Egypt but this was halted after a few days because of a shortage of supplies, particularly petrol and oil, as a result of the high percentage of sinkings of Axis ships by aircraft and submarines based on Malta.

The British forces struck at El Alamein on 23 October and commenced their advance westwards, eventually to link up with the Anglo-U.S. forces which had landed in North Africa on November 8. By then the last enemy offensive on Malta by 214 German aircraft, of which 156 were

bombers, together with 163 Italian, of which 77 were bombers, between October 11-24, had been totally defeated by the Royal Air Force so that on 20 November in Operation Stonehenge four freighters brought 35,000 tons of supplies without incident from Alexandria and in December Operation Portcullis saw three ships safely deliver 55,000 tons.

In the meantime the fast minelayers *Welshman* and *Manxman* as well as submarines had brought fuel, food, ammunition and other supplies on individual runs.

The 'Times of Malta' had started a Convoy Fund which raised £7,525 15s. by

October 15 when £1,000 were distributed to the Sailors' Fund of the British Sailors Society, £5,525 15s. to the Prince of Wales Sea Training Hostel for boys of the Merchant Navy in Limehouse, London, founded in 1920, and £1,000 to the Royal Artillery Benevolent Fund in appreciation of the sacrifices of the men of the Royal Regiment of Artillery who had died manning the light anti-aircraft guns on the merchant ships.

The Italians claimed the material advantage in the *Battaglia di Mezzo Agosto* for the losses inflicted on merchant ships and warships by their Regia Aeronautica and the submarines and fast surface craft, but in the end the British obtained a strategic victory when Malta was relieved and fought on.

Ohio was towed to Kalkara Creek where she settled on the shallow seabed and broke in half. The after part with the bridge above water served as the headquarters of the Royal Yugoslav Navy. In September 1946 she was towed out to sea and sunk by gunfire.

Three of the merchant ships which made it to Malta survived the war.

Port Chalmers had previously taken part in Operation Substance to Malta in July 1941, her cargo including 2,000 tons of aviation spirit. She was the only ship in Operation Pedestal to reach Malta undamaged. She left Malta in September, 1942, making a dash to Port Said and sailing through the Suez Canal, round the Cape of Good Hope to the United States. She continued to participate in a number of convoys. By 1965 she had outlived her time and after a farewell luncheon and reunion of Malta convoy veterans at the King George V Dock in London, she sailed on her 66th voyage to New Zealand and then proceeded to Japan to the breakers' yard.

Brisbane Star survived the war and in 1959 transferred to the Blue Star Line. She was broken up in Japan in 1963.

Rochester Castle remained in Malta till December 1942 for repairs, then made a dash to Alexandria. She sailed round the Cape to New York and returned to the United Kingdom with a cargo of frozen meat. She had a long life and was eventually broken up in 1970.

The fourth, *Melbourne Star*, was sunk by a U-Boat, 480 miles south of Bermuda on 2 April, 1943. The master, 72 crew, many of them Pedestal veterans, 11 gunners and 31 passengers bound for Australia via the Panama Canal were lost. There were only four survivors found drifting on a raft 30 days later.

Convoys following Pedestal were unloaded under floodlights

VETERANS' REUNION

There has always been a spirit of comraderie between all those who in some way were connected with Operation Pedestal.

Captain Desmond Dickens, who had been a young apprentice in *Dorset* and was rescued by the destroyer H.M.S. *Bramham*, organized reunions in 1967, 1980 and 1992 from his office as a Captain in Trinity House, London, (founded in 1514), the corporation that is responsible for the provision and maintenance of maritime communications in British territorial waters, and was. Eventually these gatherings were to lead to the setting up of the George Cross Island Association to embrace all those in the three Services, the Merchant Navy and also civilians who in some way or other participated in the siege.

Admiral of the Fleet Lord Lewin of Greenwich became its president. He had been a sub-lieutenant in H.M.S. *Ashanti* during Pedestal and by the time the G.C. Association was set up in 1987 he had retired from the Royal Navy having been First Sea Lord and eventually Chief of the Defence Staff. His resolution in the discussions with the Maltese

Signed by Pedestal veterans

100 Brit servicemen return to Malta 60 years after saving island

Why I must thank a plank

A PLANK helped me write this. Without that bit of 4x2 I wouldn't be here, writes **Rob Dalton**.

In August 1942 my dad Les was a 21-year-old signals coder on HMS Eagle, an aircraft carrier protecting Pedestal.

At 1pm on the 11th he was below deck when a German sub fired a salvo of four torpedoes at the ship.

Les recalls: "They blew out the side and she began listing. I grabbed what I thought was my lifejacket and headed for the stairs — only to find that in the confusion I'd picked up my gas mask holder."

With seconds to spare he returned and

SURVIVOR . . . Les today

found his lifebelt before leaping into the water with hundreds of crewmates.

Just six minutes after the first torpedo struck, Eagle slipped to the bottom of the Med, taking more than 200 sailors with her.

Luckily for Les, up popped that plank which he clung to until he was picked up by destroyer HMS Laforey.

"I wept as I saw you go down," said many of the reunion veterans to my dad.

Dad, from Sheffield but now living in Gloucester, has never dwelt on the sinking, despite the trauma of losing so many mates.

He simply says: "We couldn't let Hitler get away with it."

THESE immaculately turned-out elderly gents, blazer buttons glinting in the sun, may look like pensioners on a day trip.

But the rows of medals quickly give the game away — they are true heroes.

The 100 former Royal Navy and merchant seamen are lined up, as ramrod-straight as the march of time allows, on the steps of the official residence of the Prime Minister of Malta.

They were marking 60 years since their life-saving convoy of fuel, arms and food fought its way through a ferocious Nazi blockade to relieve a beleaguered garrison isle that had been under a two-year siege.

Their mission, Operation Pedestal, saved an island, a country and the free world from Hitler and his fascist crony Mussolini, whose hundreds of bombers were just 60 miles away in Sicily.

Of the 14 fast merchant ships that ran the gauntlet of constant air and sea attack when Operation Pedestal left Gibraltar on August 10 1942 just FIVE made it through to the Grand Harbour of Malta's capital Valletta five days later. Four Royal Navy warships were also sunk — more than 500

BY ROB DALTON

The final ship to arrive was the convoy's most vital vessel — the 9,000-ton US tanker Ohio, requisitioned from Texaco for Britain's last bid to reach the 300,000 starving islanders and Allied aircrew sailors and soldiers.

Her cargo of engine oil and aviation fuel was all that could prevent Malta's surrender within days. No fuel meant no fighter defence against an Axis invasion.

As Britain's wartime leader Winston Churchill later stated, the fall of Malta would have triggered the loss of the Med.

Swept

Hitler's by now unopposed armies would then have swept through North Africa and the Middle East and Europe would have stayed in Axis hands. Game over.

Little had Geordie seaman Allan Shaw first realised what a momentous part he and his Ohio shipmates were to play in history.

The sinking, holed, engineless hulk was nudged into the bomb-damaged harbour with two destroyers lashed to her side to keep her afloat and a third, HMS Ledbury, "steering" from astern until tugs took over. Then thou-

emerged from their warren of air raid shelters Allan, now 79, of Blyth, Northumberland, recalled. "It was an amazing sight — all these people waving white handkerchiefs to greet us. The reception they gave us was fantastic."

Sixty years on, the welcome which the hundred heroes of Pedestal received on their return to Malta was equally enthusiastic.

It was also quite humbling for me, the only newspaper journalist present and a mere 40-something who has fortunately never known the horrors of war.

The still grateful Maltese government, with the help of Maltese militaria buff Simon Cousens, had

SO MOVING . . . veteran Allan Savage, left, weeps as a ship re-enacts SS Ohio's arrival in Malta in 1942

for Pedestal veterans. The actual anniversary of the arrival, August 15, was ruled out because high summer in Malta would have been too hot for the survivors.

The youngest is now 77. The oldest is William Turner, former sergeon commander on bombed carrier HMS Indomitable. Spritely William flew in from Britain by himself — well, he is only 97.

Simon traced more than 200 of the 25,000 men who formed the original convoy and its escort of 64 carriers, battleships, cruisers and smaller Navy ships.

Of these, 100 were able to make the all expenses paid trip, several braving the journey despite suffer-

chairs Air Malta helped fly them in from all over the world.

At every public event of the week Maltese young and old politely pestered the sailors for autographs. They even stood next to them for a photo as the ship's bell from their saviour SS Ohio was returned to the island for the first time since the war.

Triumph

Then came the most emotional event of a highly-charged week of concerts, wreath-laying and museum visits.

Thousand of locals, headed by President Guido de Marco, plus the British High Commissioner and Ark Royal's commanding officers, joined the veterans and accompanying families at a spectacular harbourside re-enactment of the island's siege — and Pedestal's triumph.

Hundreds of actors retold the story, accompanied by wartime radio broadcasts, ear-splitting bomb explosions and some gutsy humour that got Malta through a blitz worse than anything London experienced.

The best was to come. Right on

conflict, the aircraft carrier's crew diverted to Malta to attend the celebrations honouring the heroes of Operation Pedestal.

The reunion was also a chance for reconciliation, with the presence of former Luftwaffe bomber pilot Georg Vougerel, complete with Iron Cross wartime German bravery medal, and his comrade Alfred Partzsch.

Schoolchildren were driven by awe-struck parents to our hotel to quiz the veterans about their wartime experiences and to show their charmingly naive crayon drawings of an air raid, or a ship being sunk.

Britain's biggest warship, HMS Ark Royal, was among the big guns who had come to pay respects to the war veterans.

The huge ship had been on exercise in the Mediterranean, a move hissed by military observers, to a possible strike against Iraqi leader Saddam Hussein. But in the mid-

limped round the headland into harbour stark against the gathering dusk, lashed to tugs The Ohio was back Malta was saved again.

Sixty years on young eyes which had unflinchingly witnessed wartime horrors no grown man should ever see, finally dissolved into tears.

Allan Savage served on the destroyer HMS Penn which towed the dying Ohio through the final mine-laced miles to that same Valletta anchorage six decades ago.

He was one of many who wept as he saw her modern-day equivalent arrive again.

The real ship is in two pieces on the sea bed, having broken her back just minutes after the last drop of precious fuel was pumped off, her duty done.

Tears for the memories, probably. For lost comrades, certainly — and perhaps for another group of Our Boys who may also soon have to stand up to an evil despot. The last-chance nature of this reunion was sadly emphasised when two of the veterans I had the immense pleasure of meeting died within days of returning to the UK.

Their determination to attend the reunion had been at great as their heroism in getting through to Malta

---

REPORTING THE PEDESTAL REUNIONS

Emotion-laden *Malta Invicta* reunion in London

by John A. Mizzi

PRESENTATION of Operation Pedestal print at Buckingham Palace, from left: Prince Philip, Romina Cusens, Doris Cusens, Mr and Mrs Edwin Galea, Tim Cusens, Chris Cusens and Simon Cusens

RESCUER AND RESCUED reunited after 60 years: Charles Henry Walker, GC (note the medal) of HMS Ledbury is unexpectedly reunited with the 'boy' he remembers saving, Aràn Burnett of the Waimarama, meeting him for the first time since the rescue on 13th August 1942. The George Cross was awarded to Walker for his bravery in jumping in and rescuing a handful of survivors from a blazing sea during the Santa Marija Convoy.

OFFICIAL PHOTOGRAPH of the Malta Invicta 1942 reunion (enlarged and autographed by all veterans present). This was an ideal photo to use for the event as it shows a colonial figure (Queen Victoria seated on her throne, victorious and proud) amid the devastation with islanders going about their business notwithstanding the hardship.

SIMON CUSENS presents a print of the Ohio to Dr Bonello Du Puis (John A. Mizzi)

A LIGHT-HEARTED moment as Dr Bonello Du Puis presents a scroll of the Freedom of Valletta to one of the Pedestal veterans (John A. Mizzi)

GROUP PHOTOGRAPH on the steps of St Paul's Cathedral, London: front row: Simon Cusens and Dr George Bonello Du Puis, Maltese High Commissioner in London, and some of the Malta Invicta reunion are seen with some of the veterans who attended

A SECTION of the group at the Malta Invicta reunion held at the Victory Services Club, Marble Arch, London

EXPLAINING the details of the print later presented to Dr Bonello Du Puis — from left: Simon Cusens, Edwin Galea, the artist, and Dr Bonello Du Puis

Prince Philip, Duke of Edinburgh, is presented by Simon Cusens with the 60th anniversary painting by artist Edwin Galea (centre) at Buckingham Palace

authorities resulted in the erection of the Siege Bell Memorial.

In 2001 Simon Cusens, then 33 years old, and an amateur researcher, realized the significance of the *Santa Marija* Convoy, and started to track down the survivors and even wrote to the Prime Minister of Malta, Dr. E. Fenech Adami, suggesting Malta hosts the 60th anniversary reunion and invites all the survivors on an all expenses paid trip.

He had by then located 250 veterans, including a few Germans and Italians. 105 veterans accepted the invitation, some travelling in September 2002 from as far afield as the United States, Australia and New Zealand, despite their advanced age. The Maltese Government acted as the host and Cusens ran the project, organizing a re-enactment of *Ohio's* arrival in Grand Harbour and supporting with pride the decision to confer the honorary citizenship of the city of Valletta on the veterans.

Maltese maritime artist Edwin Galea painted a special commemorative painting of the arrival of *Ohio* which was made available to the veterans and others, including a special personal presentation to the Duke of Edinburgh at Buckingham Palace.

The following year Cusens organized another reunion, this time at the Victory Services Club at Marble Arch, London, attended by 100 veterans. Cusen had a trump card up his sleeve. He had befriended Charles Walker of H.M.S. *Ledbury* who had been awarded the Albert Medal (later changed to the George Cross) for saving the life of a young seaman from the conflagration of the *Waimarama*, and knew that rescuer and rescued had never met. He located the not-so-young man, Alan Bennett, in Palm Desert, California, and flew him to London for an emotional meeting between the two.

Cusens has remained active as a link between the veterans, now sadly depleted, and has in the process amassed an archive of personal stories, memorabilia, documents and other aspects of the operation that is unique.

Every year he helps in the organization of a commemorative ceremony by the Apostleship of the Sea which is held at the Valletta Waterfront that has become a national event of thanksgiving for the *Santa Marija* Convoy.

Charles Walker breaks down in tears as he meets for the first time in 61 years, Alan Bennett, the 18-year-old he had saved from the burning *Waimarama*. Simon Cusens, who had brought them together is in the centre, with Dr George Bonello Dupuis, the Malta High Commissioner in London, at left

RE-ENACTING THE ARRIVAL OF OHIO FOR THE 60TH ANNIVERSARY COMMEMORATION HELD IN GRAND HARBOUR IN SEPTEMBER 2002

HONORARY CITIZENS OF VALLETTA

The title of Honorary Citizen of Valletta was conferred on those who participated in Operation Pedestal during the reunion in Malta in September 2002. In his address at the ceremony, the Mayor, Paul Borg Olivier, said:

We give Thee thanks Almighty God.

This was the simple prayer of all those who stood at the foot of the unbeaten bastions, on the ramparts of the dauntless Fort St. Elmo, on the dry shores of the Grand Harbour and on the bare roof tops of the shattered homes in Valletta and the Three Cities as they emotionally greeted the convoy ships sailing into the harbour in that month of August 1942.

It is a great pleasure and honour for me, as Mayor of Valletta, and on behalf of my colleague councillors and all the people of Valletta, to welcome you to Malta on the occasion of the 60th anniversary of Operation Pedestal.

May I point out from the start that Malta's gratitude and indebtedness to you and all your colleagues are infinite.

Two veterans, Raymond Morton (right) and Allan Shaw (left), both of *Ohio,* near *Ohio's* bell. The ringing of the original *Ohio* bell, during the 60th anniversary celebrations in September 2002, marked the opening of an eventful week of tributes and activities. The bell had been borrowed from the headquarters ship *Wellington,* seat of the Honorable Company of Master Mariners, to whom it had been bequeathed by Captain Mason

The passage of time will never strike off our memory of this glorious event, for your suffering was our suffering and your hopes were our hopes, and guided by the noble virtues of courage, perseverance and fortitude, to quote Winston Churchill, "the strength of Malta revived."

I am not a witness to the siege, of course, my age gives me away. I have never felt the suffering of hunger, the yelling of sirens, the blasts of bombs and the fear of dying out at sea away from my family. These must have been your thoughts and feelings as they must have been of all those who experienced those bitter moments of distress. It appeared that this was the beginning of the end for Malta.

Yet I am human, so allow me to share with you my grief for all those who died at sea or on land to give me and many others the meaning of life.

We stand here today at the St. James Cavalier, the former N.A.A.F.I. as all of you know it, in remembrance of one of one of Malta's most difficult yet glorious moments – a turning point in our history.

We stand here today to give homage to those who gave their lives for others and to honour you, the survivors oif Operation Pedestal, for the outstanding noble virtues you have shown throughout your service.

During this operation, the Ohio alone was singled out, ferociously attacked by the enemy. She was torpedoed and holed, fire broke out, her boilers blew up and her engines failed. She was twice abandoned and twice reboarded. Repeated attempts to tow failed, but the tanker did not sink. Ohio, with the help of all the other vessels in the operation shaped the fate of Malta.

The ships' resistance was equalled by the power of the seamen who, with no time for food and rest, manned the crippled ships to port. For everybody then it was felt that this was the beginning of the end of war this time. War is not a means of showing people how to get what they want. World War II was a terrible experience by means of which men, women and children, it is hoped, have learnt to want what is worth having and cherishing.

Standing battered and bloodied, Operation Pedestal and Malta made a great history and paved the way to victory over the forces of the Third Reich. It is for these reasons that the Valletta City local government has agreed to confer, for the first time, the title of HONORARY CITIZENS OF VALLETTA *to you present and to others in absentia.*

FACING THE MUSIC

Lieutenant John "Junior" Young was a Fleet Air Arm pilot flying from H.M.S. Indomitable. In a letter to the author he described how he evaded death when 14 off-duty pilots and observers in the carrier's wardroom were killed when she was hit and near missed by a number of bombs at about 7.30 p.m. on 11 August.

During this time I was one of five officers who played the piano for my own amusement in the wardroom. On 13 August, after three days evading torpedoes and bombs, I completed two sorties in a Sea Hurricane of 880 Squadron and retired to the wardroom which was empty to play the piano. After half an hour I was interrupted by a friend who claimed it was his turn to play the piano and furthermore there was a Hurricane awaiting a pilot. I left for the flight-deck and was soon airborne. I had reached only 1,000 feet when a squadron of German Stukas dive-bombed *Indomitable* scoring several direct hits. One bomb exploded in the wardroom blowing up piano and player. Strangely my music, Mozart Sonatas, survived but burned at the edges! I have them still.

John Young with two of his famous breed of horses which drew drays, carriages delivering beer barrels

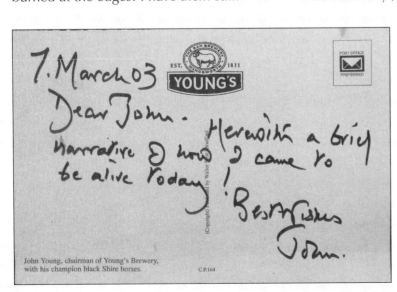

7. March 03

Dear John.

Herewith a brief narrative of how I came to be alive Today!

Best wishes

John.

John Young, chairman of Young's Brewery, with his champion black Shire horses.   C.P.164

John Young left the Navy in 1947 and in 1962 succeeded his father William as chairman of the family brewery firm, Young's, of Wandsworth, London, which among other beer-related enterprises, operated over 200 pubs. He held this post for 44 years, till his death in 2006.

'ULTRA' REVELATIONS

Ultra was the name given to the system which intercepted and decrypted the enemy's coded messages sent by wireless telegraphy via the German Enigma machines. As these messages could be scrambled, by complicated electric circuitry, into one of 150,000,000,000,000,000,000 different combinations, the system seemed to the Germans to be so absolutely undecipherable that they sent their messages, using Morse code, in plain language. Moreover, each major Service used different key settings and also a different code key for each different theatre of war. As supply requests, as well as purely military information, were passed via these Enigma machines and as the Italians, using similar C38 machines, became involved, there could be as many as 50 different key settings in operation at the same time. To increase further the security of the enemy's top secret communications, each message was apt to be sent when using a different key setting from the last.

By 1939, led by the Poles, the British, French and Polish Intelligence had got wind of the existence of the Enigma machines (which looked like rather big and clumsy typewriters) and the Poles had even managed to manufacture a reasonable facsimile of one. In September 1939 there was recognition that only another electronic machine could possibly unscramble a message sent by Enigma.

Fortunately a brilliant young Cambridge University mathematical genius, Alan Turing, proceeded to reproduce a counter-machine. His *bombe*, as it was called, was a vast calculating computer which occupied about half a fair-sized room. As silicone chips had not been invented, it used radio valves, about 1,500 of them.

This monster machine had the capability of running through, at the speed of light, all possible combinations of an intercepted enemy wireless telegraphy message until, arriving at one which was in the German language and not, like the others, an unintelligible jumble of letters.

To cope with this new system, the British took over a country house called Bletchley

The *Enigma* machine

The *bombe*, the electro-mechanical computer of enormous complexity built by Alan Turing to decode the German Enigma messages at Bletchley Park. It was 2.1 metres (7 feet) wide, 1.98 metres (6 feet 6 inches) high and 0.6 metres (2 feet) deep and weighed a ton

Park and, along with the mathematicians, they installed their best cryptanalysts and German-speaking translators. The decrypts were then sent out in English but only to the very senior commanders; also to the various ministries and to the War Cabinet. Sometime much later, the Americans were also introduced to Ultra and Bletchley Park.

Ultra had its limitations. It was of less use in Europe as it was important in the Mediterranean because it depended upon a message having to be by wireless telegraphy. Where land-lines or a courier service was used, it was obviously blind. At times some of the intercepted messages apparently were replies to questions which had been transmitted by means of other wireless telegraphy. These posed problems. In reality, all intercepts, even after having been deciphered, still required the attention of military experts: abbreviations and technical terms needed to be explained, the authority of each sender had to be known, then assessed etc, etc.

Much had to be done to extract the most from this priceless information and it was in the Balkans and Middle East, where telephone connections were poor or non-existent, that these teething problems came to light, first in Yugoslavia then in Greece/Crete. However it was only after Rommel had been moved to Africa in February 1941 that the Ultra signals became frequent and of vital importance. Then, after establishing a Special Liaison Unit to receive the signals, the commanders-in-chief in Cairo and Alexandria were regularly informed of Rommel's orders emanating from Berlin, also of Rommel's intentions as expressed by him to Berlin.

As it was firm policy not to reveal to anyone one scrap more of Ultra's background than was absolutely necessary, an early difficulty was to persuade the few recipients that the Ultra was reliable and straight from the horse's mouth. However, bit by bit, the war leaders in the Middle East and Malta came to realize that, in R.A.F. parlance, Ultra signals were "real pukka gen."

Some idea of the tight security which surrounded Ultra, can be guaged by the fact that in Malta only one person was allowed to receive Ultra intercepts. This was Charles Carnes, a former naval officer on the Reserve. He was in charge of the Naval Cipher Office at Fort St. Anglo and he had therefore at all times to let others know where he could be found day and night. It helped that he lived a blameless life!

Carnes then passed the message to the Vice-Admiral Malta. Yet, not until about 30 years after the war, did Carnes know the slightest thing about Enigma, Turing's *bombe* or even the existence of Bletchley Park. All that he knew was that Ultra messages were top secret. He presumed, as indeed most of those in Malta did, that the British had agents in the enemy's ports of embarkation, the so-called "men at the end of the pier" who were passing on the priceless details regarding all sailings of ships to North Africa and in the case of Pedestal the movements of the Italian warships.

As it was, since the Regia Marina in Rome advised by wireless telegraphy all sailings of ships, when they would depart, the route to be taken, the names and number of ships and plans of operation, the Malta Headquarters had vital information for the submarines and strike aircraft operating from the island.

However, for security reasons only those ships which could be additionally located by means which would be apparent to the enemy were to be attacked. To have done so otherwise would have given the enemy an obvious indication that his Enigma transmissions were being read. Nobody in Malta other than the Vice-Admiral Malta had any inkling about Ultra or Enigma – it is even doubtful that the Vice-Admiral Malta knew that Bletchley Park existed.

This article is reproduced from The National Newsletter *No. 29 of George Cross Island Association*

THE SURRENDER OF THE ITALIAN FLEET

The ship's company of H.M.S. *Warspite* watch the battleship *Vittorio Veneto* on her way to Malta to lead the Italian fleet surrender on 10 September, 1943

HEROES OF THE 'SANTA ELISA'

Francis A. Dales was a young cadet midshipman and Frederick August Larsen junior third officer on the American merchant ship Santa Elisa. *The story of their ordeal in Operation Pedestal was told in the U.S. Merchant Marine website.*

The *Santa Elisa* was a freighter carrying drums of high octane gasoline, one of two American ships. Heavily escorted, the convoy was under constant attack from Axis planes and submarines. Assigned the command of an anti-aircraft gun mounted on the bridge, Larsen contributed to the successful defence of his ship for three days. At 4 a.m. on the fourth day torpedo boats succeed in breaking through and two attacked from opposite sides. Sneaking in close under the cover of darkness one opened point blank with four 50 calibre machine guns, sweeping the bridge. The other fired a torpedo into the opposite side of the freighter.

Cadet Midshipman
Francis A. Dales
Santa Elisa

Third Officer
Fred Larsen
Santa Elisa

The explosion of the torpedo ignited the gasoline and the American ship was in flames. Reluctantly orders were given to abandon her. Two hours later the survivors were picked up by a British destroyer* which then proceeded to take in tow a tanker that had been bombed and could not manoeuvre, the *Ohio*, which was also American, although British-crewed.

Santa Elisa

After five hours of constant dive-bombing, the tanker was hit again. Her crew abandoned her and the destroyer was forced to cut her loose. But the cargo she carried was most important to the defence of Malta and it had to get through. The rescue destroyer and another destroyer steamed in, lashed themselves on either side of the stricken tanker and dragged her along in a determined attempt to get her to port. The tanker's decks and superstructure had been almost completely wrecked by the incessant bombardment.

But Larsen's anxiety to get into the fight caused him to take inventory of her armament. He found an anti-aircraft gun mounted abaft the stack which needed only minor repairs to put it into action. The young cadet of his own ship, Francis A. Dales, a British gunner's mate and three of his men volunteered to help him. Though the ships were then constantly under attack, they boarded the *Ohio*, repaired the gun and manned it, with Larsen taking the trainer's position and the gunner's mate

and the cadet alternating as pointers. The shackled ships, inching along and making perfect targets, were assailed by concentrated enemy air power.

All that day wave after wave of German and Italian bombers dived at them and were beaten off by a heavy barrage. Bombs straddled them, scoring near misses, but no direct hits were made until noon the next day, when the tanker finally received a bomb down her stack which blew out the bottom of her engine room. Though she continued to settle until her decks were awash, they fought her through until dusk that day brought them under the protection of the hard fighting air force of Malta.

The magnificent courage of this young third officer and cadet-midshipman constitutes a degree of heroism which will be an enduring inspiration to seamen of the United States merchant marine everywhere.

Larsen was 27, Dales 18.

'WELSHMAN' TO THE RESCUE

The fast minelayer H.M.S. *Welshman* entering Grand Harbour on one of her runs to bring supplies to Malta. In the foreground are the bombed ruins of naval headquarters at Lascaris Bastions, Valletta

THE DRAMATIC END OF 'WAIMARAMA'

Waimarama blows up within seconds after being hit on the morning of 13 August. H.M.S. *Ledbury* is visible at right steaming into the inferno.

About a dozen planes came in low from the port beam and a flight of Junkers 88s came out of the sun. A stick of bombs hit the *Waimarama* and she blew up with the biggest explosion I have ever seen. It was terrible. The flames were hundreds of feet high and a great expanse of sea was covered in rolling smoke and flames.

The Armiral made to me: "Survivors, but don't go into the flames." I took the ship to the edge of the flames but did not think anyone could have survived. As we approached there were heads bobbing about in the water, waving arms and faces blackened with oil. I slipped the whaler, with Mr. Musham*, our gunner, (the terror of Whale Island Gunnery School parade ground) in command and left him

astern to gather in the more distant survivors. I encouraged with the loud hailer those we passed, saying I must get the ones near the fire first, and they shouted back:"That's all right" and "Don't forget the diver."

The flames were spreading outward over the sea, even to windward, and it was a grim race to get the ship stopped in position to pick up the men in the water before the flames reached them.

… all sorts of people were jumping over the side with lines and bringing survivors, some seriously burned, to the landing nets.

As we moved in and out of the flames and smoke, scattered S 84 bombers dropped what we thought were sort of floating mines by parachute (we had seen these for the first time

* Mr C. E. Musham was awarded the Distinguished Service Cross.

Waimarama

in the big attack on the previous evening)** but we were too busy to take much notice, except to shoot at the planes.

Finally, I could see no one left in the water and was just about to return thankfully to the whaler when the coxswain reported up the voice pipe: "There's a man on a raft in the flames." He had only a small porthole looking ahead, but through some vagary of the smoke he was able to see this man, though from the bridge all we could see was thick smoke and flames.

I hesitated, wishing to ignore what he reported. Then I wondered if the ship would blow up if we went right into the heat. The density of the smoke changed and I saw a man sitting on some debris surrounded by leaping flames, and as he raised his arm to us, I took the ship in and shouted to Number One: "For Christ's sake, be quick!"

The flames were higher than the mast and the roaring noise and choking fumes were all around us. "Jesus," said Yeoman, (who had been forbidden to go over the side) "It's just like a film!"

The cook*** had come out of his galley aft, saw the man, took off his apron, kicked off his boots and over he went after him. He got to the raft, dragged him off and swam with him to the after landing net.

I felt I could not wait any longer and called through the loud hailer: "Hold on like hell.

I'm going astern." We came out fast astern and I was sure the cook and the man would have been washed away, but he had one arm round the man's neck and the other through the net and had held on. We whipped them in, picked up Guns and his collection in the whaler and wandered what to do.

We had been two hours picking up 45 survivors (one of whom was dead) and so we were 30 miles astern of the convoy and getting desperately short of fuel if we were to go to Malta and then back to the tanker off Algiers.

I told the Admiral I was 30 miles astern and set off to rejoin the convoy. At 10.50 we

Lieut. Cdr. Roger Hill, captain of H.M.S. *Ledbury*

**

Motobombas, aerial torpedoes dropped by parachute which ran in circles.

*** Charles Henry Walker was awarded the Albert Medal, later converted to the George Cross

had a private attack all to ourselves by seven Ju88s and we had the usual near misses, whilst David reported shooting one plane down.

Another sadness now hit us, since we found we had survivors on board not only from the *Waimarama* but also the *Melbourne Star*... All we had from the two was 44.

Ledbury joined the group shepherding *Ohio* some 100 miles from Malta.

I asked for volunteers to tow *Ohio* from the survivors we had picked up from the fire, and all the men who were not injured or badly shocked said they would go. I thought this was just about the bravest act I had ever known. If *Ohio* was hit she would go up even higher than the merchant ships they had been on and they would not have a chance. I wanted particularly merchant seamen to handle the winch and gear on the *Ohio*, which would be different from navy winches. The bo'sun of the *Waimarama* was among the survivors and how we would have got on without him I just do not know.

Ohio was dragged slowly forward by *Ledbury*, *Penn*, and *Rye* under air attack after air attack. Various efforts were made to tow the tanker to Malta during the evening and night and eventually she was bodily manoeuvred into Grand Harbour.

At daylight I walked round the upper deck. The sleeping bodies of the sailors lay sprawled and hunched in their duffel coats. The friends' legs or backs made pillows. Through the growth of beard and the sunburn their faces looked so young and peaceful. I felt a great surge of affection and pride for what they had achieved and deep gratitude that we had come through it all without a casualty.

Destroyer Captain by Roger Hill,
(William Kimber) 1975

Lieut. H.A.J. Hollings, the First Lieutenant of Ledbury, in his report after the Operation wrote:

... there only remained one man on the raft and he was right on the edge of the flames and could not help himself. The captain pushed the bows right up to the edge of the flames and I asked for a volunteer to go over and get a line onto the man. Ord Sea (Reginald) Sida* volunteered and while I held a couple of lines, he jumped over the side. I then gave him one of the lines for himself and the other for the survivor and he pushed his way through the wreckage of the raft. After a lot of trouble he got the line round the man and we were able to pull them both along to the rescue nets and get them in. There was also a corpse floating there and that, too, was pulled in just in case. Then we went back to the whaler which by now had about 20 survivors aboard. We got them on board, hoisted the whaler and set off after the convoy now some 20 miles ahead. I went down below getting the survivors settled down and taking their names. It was now that I found we had the men from two separate ships, the *Waimarama* and the *Melbourne Star*. Final count showed 18 from *Waimarama* and 24 from *Melbourne Star* with one dead man, I think he was a gunner from *Melbourne Star*.

* Ord Sea Reginald Sida, was awarded the Distinguished Service Medal

THE 'OHIO' BIBLE

Roy Morton and his bible recovered from *Ohio*

Ray Morton was 18 when he joined *Ohio* as assistant steward for Operation Pedestal. On 10 August he was at action stations on the machine-gun on the boat deck when at 6 p.m. *Ohio* was torpedoed.

He and three others were thrown in the sea and were picked up three hours later by the destroyer *Bicester*. He could not swim but was kept afloat by his life-jacket. A sailor from the destroyer jumped into the sea and helped him aboard with a heaving line. He was put ashore at Gibraltar a few days later on the return of the escort ships of Operation Pedestal.

He arrived home over a month later. One day his vicar called at his home with his bible which he had left in *Ohio*. It had been sent to him through the Bible and Tract Society to whom it had been sent, with a request for him to contact the vicar "and for him to return the book to the bereaved parents." Inside was a letter written by Able Seaman C.F. Cliffe to explain that he himself had been rescued by one of the escorting destroyers which had assisted to tow *Ohio*. Cliff wrote: "Late one afternoon I went on board the tanker to have a look at the damage by enemy bombs, which had literally reduced the crew's quarters to a shambles. Searching among the debris for odds and ends, such as a piece of soap to wash with, or an old pair of trousers, to replace our dirty ones which we had damaged during rescue work, I picked up the Bible and book (by Mr Lionel Fletcher) in the cabin evidently occupied by Raymond. I had lost my own Bible so I kept this copy till such times as I could purchase a new one. Thinking that the boy's parents would be interested to know the circumstances in which the books were recovered, I am writing to ask you if you would kindly forward the books on to them."

In September 2002 Morton donated the book to Simon Cusens who had helped him to come to Malta from Queensland, Australia, for the 60th Anniversary Reunion. Morton at 88 is one of the few survivors of Operation Pedestal still alive.

THE SAGA OF 'BRISBANE STAR'

Captain Riley Master of the Brisbane Star, *had very strong opinions on the actions of his crew and openly expressed his views in writing, "which I have thought should be kept apart from the main report."*

On the 13th instant about 9 a.m. I was approached very respectfully by Mr. Sherratt, Senior 2nd. Engineer, and Mr. Weller, Chief Ref. Engineer. They stated they were representing their department and wanted to know would I let them know my intentions. I informed them that my intentions were to hug the coast until dark and then break away for

Malta. I asked them what was their worry. They replied that the recent experiences has brought their nerves to breaking point and some of the younger ones had reached the verge of tears. I sympathized with them over the rotten job it must be down below when events were happening on top but informed them my duty was clear and the job was to get the ship to Malta and I promised them that if the worst did happen they would not be forgotten. They thanked me and left quite satisfied.

Towards 11 a.m. a deputation of three from the greasers' department approached me

Brisbane Star entering Grand Harbour at 3.30 p.m. on 14 August

Distinguished Service Order

Bronze Cross - Boy Scouts Association

The awards and medals of Captain Riley:
Distinguished Service Order
Silver Cross for Gallantry of the Boy Scouts
Association for saving a boy from drowning
on 6 June, 1909
British War Medal 1914-18
Mercantile Service Medal 1914-18
1939-45 Star
Africa Star
Pacific Star
War Medal 1939-45

on the bridge and asked me would I let them what I was going to do. I informed them that we were bound for Malta. This did not have their approval but they soon left.

Shortly after 1 p.m. another three persons from the forecastle approached me and wanted to know what I intended to do and these three were also informed that we were bound for Malta. They wanted to know would I go without an escort and they were informed that such a decision would be made later. They then wanted to know couldn't I proceed with a skeleton crew and together with their many ideas of what I should do they would have talked for ever. They were therefore dismissed.

About 4 p.m. once again three seamen approached and they stated they represented the deck, greasers' and stewards' departments. They had come along to argue that I scuttle the ship and advanced their argument that if the *Graf Spee* could scuttle herself I was in a position much more entitled to. Like the last three, on this theme and several other petty ones, they would have occupied my time for years and so they were dismissed but left the

bridge stating that they would sooner swim ashore than come along.

During the day I was approached a number of times by individuals who informed me the ship was settling down by the head, some said quickly, some went so far as to say that standing on the poop it could be watched and that being on the main deck it was most noticeable. They were each and all informed that they were imagining things and that the facts of the position were otherwise.

Leaving the above, I would state that about 3 p.m. this day, two points forward of the port beam I observed a suspicious streak in the water. At the inner end of the streak I even thought I saw a periscope for a few seconds and I mentioned this to our liaison officer, Lieut. Symes, who was standing by me. I would take this opportunity to add that Lieut. Symes' services were quite valuable and much appreciated throughout. He could see nothing suspicious but I starboarded to bring the vessel closer inshore, as at this time we were some three to four miles off the coast, and this action also put the streak abaft the beam.

The shattered bows of *Brisbane Star* on arrival in Grand Harbour

After this there was a submarine report from aft and for the next hour there were several reports from aft to the effect that we were being followed by a submarine and some of the reports were that the periscope had been sighted, but by this time I could see nothing suspicious. Most people were inclined to accept the reports as "dead certs" and quite a number are of that opinion now. It was at this period that Lieut. Symes approached me and stated that my chances of getting to Malta were nil for as soon as I left the coast the submarine reported to be following would put three torpedoes into us and we would be blown sky high. He added that as I couldn't save the ship and as I could at least save the lives on board the time had come for me to scuttle. The Sea Transport Officer, Lieut. Eva, was also of this opinion.

Fortunately, it so happens I could not and would not agree. I finally consulted with Mr. White, Chief Officer, and though Mr. White throughout was agreeable to any of my decisions, he thought there was a lot in what Lieut. Symes had stated and what Lieut. Eva had thought, too. I am pleased to add that their opinions were short lived and they were with me again in next to no time.

The atmosphere, however, was much against me and so at this time I decided to muster all hands amidships and call for volunteers. It was at this time also that we received a signal from Malta that Beaufighters would meet us in the morning.

When the hands were mustered, I left the bridge but on the way down I changed my mind and decided not to call for volunteers. I told the crowd that Beaufighters would escort us in the morning but meantime we were bound for Malta. There were a few dissident voices that shouted they were going to swim ashore, but mostly it was accepted quite calmly, and so Mr. Nicol, Chief Engineer, remarked later they all seemed quite relieved about the whole situation and returned to their duties. From there on the behaviour of everyone was of the highest order.

NAVAL OFFICER'S REPORT

Lieutenant E.D. Symes was the senior naval officer on board Brisbane Star *and a confidant of Captain Riley. He submitted a report to the Vice-Admiral Malta within 24 hours of the freighter's arrival. He described the weather during the trip as "fine and clear, the wind causing sufficient white horses on this day (11 August) to conceal a submarine's periscope feather." He records the early attacks on the convoy, the sinking of* H.M.S. Eagle *and the increasing air attacks on the ships, an attack on* Victorious, *the loss of* Deucalion, *the torpedoing of* Nigeria, Cairo *and* Ohio, *the sinking of* Empire Hope *and* Clan Ferguson. *He then recounts how his ship was hit.*

The same Ju88 bomber that torpedoed *Clan Ferguson* torpedoed us in the bow at 8.58 p.m. It entered the port side of the forepeak and blew in the forward bulkhead flooding No. 1 hold and flooding nine feet, subsequently ten feet six inches, of No.1 'tween decks. It rendered the anchors and cables useless and blew our stem piece out at the waterline. Both paravanes remained towing from the A frame and were subsequently recovered. The ship stopped with the explosion but was immediately got under way again by the captain at 5 knots.

The attack was over by this time and the ship proceeded on a 180 degrees course in the wake of the cruisers. All hands behaved very well, and particularly the captain. There were no casualties.

It was decided then, that as we could not make more than 10 knots, we had best leave the convoy to whom we would be only a lame duck, make our way down the Tunisian channel down the coast till we reached Monastir, and then strike across to Malta during the night, and hope the enemy would be too busy with the convoy to take much notice of us. There were many points in

favour of the plan, and risks have to be taken to obtain success in war.

Accordingly we turned south and proceeded along close inshore, and were passed by all of the remaining ships in the convoy, including to our surprise, the tanker *Ohio*. A destroyer attempted to round us up, so we advised him of our intentions and proceeded alone. As conjectured, by the time we reached Kelibia Point, the E-boats had left and we were not troubled by them. We sighted a darkened vessel, either submarine or small patrol vessel lying inshore of us, apparently at anchor, but it took no action.

On passing through position R, we passed the *Glenorchy* evidently sinking, with a destroyer standing by. She exploded, or was torpedoed about 9 p.m. the following morning, as we could see her smoke on the horizon. As we passed close inshore, we sighted a big warship, which I took to be either a big French destroyer or an Italian light cruiser, heading south, but probably not under way, as we passed her at five knots. From her silhouette, I am almost certain she was Italian* and definitely not British. She did not molest us and I did not send an enemy report as I considered it more important that we should get by without being D/F'ed, and as our forces were away to the eastward by then. However, everything was ready to send one as soon as she opened fire. We did not observe her when daylight came.

Firing was heard and starshells fired to eastward intermittently through the night.

At about 7 a.m. we were a mile off the coast and a few miles to the northward of Hammamet Bay. An Italian Caproni torpedo-bomber appeared from the southward and circled the ship at close range. We did not fire, nor did he. We were flying no ensign, but our identity must have been obvious. He then carried out a couple of dummy torpedo attacks, and as we did not fire, disappeared to the northward. He reappeared later, as we were off Hammamet, and this time came straight at the ship. We turned, but not in time, and held our fire. He passed about fifty feet overhead, circled over the town,

* The Italian destroyer *Malocello* laying mines

circled us twice again, and disappeared to the southward. As the captain stated, he was a gentleman, and observed the international rules of war. However, we waited the whole day for a Teutonic gentleman to arrive and deliver the coup de grace, but none came.

We circled off Hammamet and the coast to the north during the morning and then proceeded to pass south of Monastir at 5 knots. We decide that perhaps the Italian gentleman's conscience might be stricken if we were off a French town and he tried to torpedo us.

An amusing exchange of signals took place here, as follows:

HAMMAMET: *You should hoist your signal letters.*

BRISBANE STAR: *Please excuse me.*

HAMMAMET: *You should anchor.*

BRISBANE STAR: *My anchors are fouled, I cannot anchor.*

HAMMAMET: *You appear to be dragging your bow and stern anchors.*

BRISBANE STAR: *I have no stern anchor.*

HAMMAMET: *You should anchor immediately.*

BRISBANE STAR: *I cannot anchor, my anchors are fouled.*

HAMMAMET: *Do you require salvage or rescue?*

BRISBANE STAR: *No.*

HAMMAMET: *It is not safe to go too fast.*

We then steered away still at 5 knots.

During the forenoon , after being sighted by the Italian bomber I made a signal on the convoy wave and commercial wave to Malta, announcing our intentions, without getting any reply.

During the afternoon of this day, 13 August, we steamed south to Susa Bay. I made a further signal to Malta on receiving a reply to the first one, as soon as we left the bay. Although neither myself nor the captain saw anything, a periscope was often reported and a track definitely seen astern. This caused the crew a certain amount of mental anxiety.

It had been decided to leave the coast at dusk, owing to submarines and aircraft, which we expected to attack us as soon as we left territorial waters, but on receipt of

Malta's acknowledgement, the solution was obvious.

Just as we turned east and increased speed, a launch came out of Susa harbour and ordered us to stop. We proceeded at 10 knots until a shot fell 10 yards off our bow. We therefore stopped and were boarded . They attempted to make the captain steam the ship into port, but he very diplomatically refused, and they gave us their best wishes, noted down carefully our course and time of leaving, and the damage to the bows. We landed one casualty who was not expected to live.

We proceeded at oue maximum speed, 10 knots, zig-zagging due east, until out of sight of land. It was 7.30 p.m. when we passed abeam of the Monastir Cape. Any submarine therefore had to keep below the surface until dark and could not catch us up. However, at 9.30 p.m. an enemy submarine was picked up very close at hand reporting a vessel and asking for aircraft. (My telegraphist had previously done much listening in on their waves and consequently could recognize the procedure). Due to lack of power, atmospherics and interference, W/T signals could not be received properly. We maintained strict silence until within sight of Malta.

At 9.30 p.m. we altered course to the southward and, at 10 p.m. when it was dark, altered course again to the southward to pass 10 miles south of Lampedusa.

A good lookout was kept, but nothing was sighted. However, just before daylight we again picked up an enemy submarine reporting a vessel and asking for an aircraft. We took his D/F bearing -207 degrees, but could not see anything.

The Beaufighter joined us at 6.30 a.m. and from then on we had fighter escort. A Ju88 bomber appeared from the south at 7.30 and passed about 20 feet above our funnel. We opened up and repeatedly hit him, but after nearly crashing into the starboard side, he flew away with smoke from his engines close above the water, followed by a Beaufighter. He dropped a heavy delay action bomb about 10 feet way abreast our funnel and jettisoned another on the further side.

About half an hour later an Italian Caproni torpedo-bomber approached from

Brisbane Star unloading her cargo soon after her arrival in Grand Harbour

the south. We turned stern on, and as he was getting into position to attack, a Beaufighter came up on his tail and shot him down into the water.

We arrived safely at Malta at 3.30 p.m. 14 August, and were berthed at No. 7 berth by 4.15.

There were no brilliant feats of courage or devotion to duty, everyone from the captain down to the deckhand did their duty in the face of the enemy as was expected of them... However Captain F.N. Riley, Blue Star Line, certainly deserves an award for his leadership and the example he inspired around him.

VICE-ADMIRAL MALTA REPORT

The Vice-Admiral Malta, Vice-Admiral Ralph Leatham, is his report on the outcome of the operation, dated 26 August, said that during the forenoon (of 13 August) he had received a signal from a ship using the call sign of the Senior Officer Force F stating that she was damaged and intending cruising in the Gulf of Hammamet during the day and crossing to Malta at 11 knots after dark and asking for suggestions. A second signal was received from another unidentified ship reporting "engine room flooded, fire."

The ships did not identify themselves and were thought to be one and the same ship. At first it was thought the ship was *Manchester* but when it was learnt the cruiser had been

sunk, she was thought to be *Kenya*. The original signal went unanswered but in the evening a further signal asked if the original signal had been received.

I therefore replied asking for the name of the ship and giving him a route but as I still thought it was *Kenya* telling him not to come to Malta unless it was impracticable for him to return to Gibraltar. Fortunately, the Master of the *Brisbane Star*, who now proved to be the unknown vessel, disregarded my advice as regards returning to Gibraltar, and after an anxious day in the Gulf of Hammamet, proceeded to Malta passing south of Lampedusa.

The Commander of the Minesweepers in *Speedy*, with the remainder of the Malta Force, sailed before dark to meet the *Ohio* which at that time was reported to be making three knots. When just clear of the entrance to the searched channels I ordered him to detach two sweepers and two motor launches to meet *Brisbane Star* at 8 a.m. next morning and escort her to Malta. *Hebe* and *Hythe* and *ML 134* and *ML 462* were detailed accordingly.

I consider that Captain Riley showed great skill and tact in dealing with the French authorities and never lost sight of his getting his object of getting his ship through to Malta. His initiative, clear thinking and determination were outstanding.

AWARDS

Several of the officers of the naval ships, including Admiral Syfret, and masters and crew members of the merchant ships were decorated.

Vice-Admiral Syfret was made a Knight Commander of the Order of the Bath "for his bravery and dauntless resolution in fighting an important convoy to Malta in the face of relentless attacks by day and night from enemy submarines, aircraft and surface forces."

Rear-Admiral Harold M. Burrough was made a Knight Commander of the Order of the British Empire.

Rear-Admiral A.L. St G. Lyster was made a Commander of the Order of the British Empire.

Captain Dudley Mason of *Ohio* was awarded the George Cross. "During the passage to Malta of an important convoy Captain Mason's ship suffered most violent onslaught. She was a focus of attack throughout and was torpedoed early one night. Although gravely damaged, her engines were kept going and the Master made a magnificent passage by hand steering and without compass. The ship's gunners helped to bring down one of the attacking aircraft. The vessel was hit again before morning, but though she did not sink, her engine was wrecked. She was then towed. The unwieldly condition of the vessel and persistent enemy attacks made progress slow, and it was uncertain whether she would remain afloat. The next day progress somehow continued and the ship reached Malta after a further night at sea. The violence of the enemy could not deter the Master from his purpose. Throughout he showed skill and courage of the highest order and it was due

Vice-Admiral
Neville Syfret

Rear-Admiral
Arthur Lyster

Rear-Admiral
H. M. Burrough

Captain Dudley Mason
Ohio

to his determination that, in spite of the most persistent enemy opposition, the vessel, with her valuable cargo, eventually reached Malta and was safely berthed."

The Albert Medal (later converted to the George Cross) was awarded to:

Petty Officer Cook Charles Henry Walker of H.M.S. *Ledbury*: "During a convoy to Malta a vessel was hit by bombs in an air attack and burst into flames fore and aft. An escorting destroyer went very close, lowered her whaler and picked up survivors from the sea. Petty Officer Cook Walker seeing a man in difficulties dived over the destroyer's side and rescued him. The heat was intense and he knew that his ship might have to turn away at any moment. Both rescued and rescuer were picked up."

Apprentice **John Sedgwick Gregson**, 18, of *Deucalion*: "The ship was set on fire by the explosion of a torpedo during an attack by enemy aircraft. The flames spread rapidly and almost immediately orders were given to abandon ship. One of the ship's gunners however was pinned under a raft. Apprentice Gregson immediately went to his assistance and help free him. The gunner had sustained severe injuries and as it was impossible to get him in a boat or to a raft he was dropped overboard. Gregson dived into the sea after him and, in the darkness, towed his hapless shipmate to a ship which picked them up, a distance of some 600 yards. But for Apprentice Gregson's gallant and determined action undertaken with complete disregard of his personal safety the injured gunner would have had little chance of survival."

The U.S. Merchant Marine Distinguished Service Medal was awarded to **Frederick August Larsen Jr**, 27, Junior Third Officer, and **Francis A. Dales**, Cadet Midshipman, of *Santa Elisa* "for heroism above and beyond the call of duty." Both also received the Grave Lines Gold Medal for Bravery.

The London Gazette of November 10, 1942 announced awards "for bravery and dauntless resolution while serving in H.M. Ships *Ashanti*, *Bramham*, *Cairo*, *Charybdis*, *Fury*, *Icarus*, *Intrepid*, *Ithuriel*, *Kenya*, *Laforey*, *Ledbury*, *Nelson*, *Nigeria*, *Pathfinder*, *Penn*, *Rodney*, *Rye*, *Somali*, *Speedy*, *Tartar*, and *Wolverine* and in H.M. Aircraft Carriers, Merchantmen and Oilers when an important convoy was fought through to Malta in the face of relentless attacks by day and night from enemy submarines, aircraft and surface forces."

Bar to the Distinguished Service Order: **Commander R.G. Onslow** (*Ashanti*), Distinguished Service Order: **Captain H.C. Bovell** (*Victorious*); **Captain R.M.J. Hutton** (*Laforey*); **Captain A. S. Russell** (*Kenya*); **Captain T.H. Troubridge** (*Indomitable*); **Cdr. H.J.A.S. Jerome** (*Speedy*); **Lieut. Cdr.**

Petty Officer Cook
Charles Henry Walker
H.M.S. *Ledbury*

Captain
F.N. Riley
Brisbane Star

Captain
R. Wren
Rochester Castle

Captain
D.R. MacFarlane
Melbourne Star

J.M. Bruen (*Indomitable*); **Lieut. Cdr. P.W. Gretton** (*Wolverine*); **Lieut. Cdr. Richard Hill** (*Ledbury*); **Lieut. Cdr. J.H. Swain** (*Penn*); **Lieut. Cdr. E.F. Baines** (*Bramham*); **Captain D.R. MacFarlane** (*Melbourne Star*); **Chief Engineer John Wyld** (*Ohio*); **Captain Richard Wren** (*Rochester Castle*); **Captain H.C. Pinkney** (*Port Chalmers*), **Captain R. Brown** (*Deucalion*), **Captain H. Gordon** (*Wairangi*); **Captain G. Williams** (*Empire Hope*); **Captain J. Tuckett** (*Dorset*); Distinguished Service Cross: **Lieut. J.A. Pearson** (*Rye*); **Lieut. D. E. Barton** (*Ohio*); **Captain D.B.C. Ralph** (*Brown Ranger*); **Chief Engineer Stanley G.L. Bentley** (*Port Chalmers*); **Second Officer Arthur Henry Dadson** (*Port Chalmers*); **Mr. C. E. Musham** (Ledbury). Various awards were made to the Fleet Air Arm aircrews including **Lieut. R.J. Cork** who shot down a number of Axis aircraft, and to Royal Navy personnel and merchant seamen for their individual courage and performance.

Walker died in July 2011 and Hill in May 2001. Their ashes were scattered at sea off Malta.

THE AIR BATTLE

LUFTWAFFE

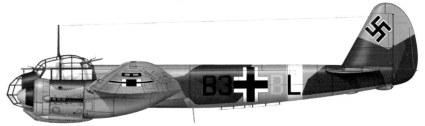

Junkers Ju 88D-4/Trop, B3+BL, I/KG 54, Gerbini (Sicily), Summer 1942

Junkers Ju 87D-1, S7+EM, 8/StG 3, Trapani (Sicily), Summer 1942

REGIA AERONAUTICA

Junkers Ju 87R-2, WrNr.7061/239-7, flown by Magg. Pil. Giuseppe Cenni, 239a Squadriglia (101º Gruppo Bombardamento a Tuffo), Gela, August 1942

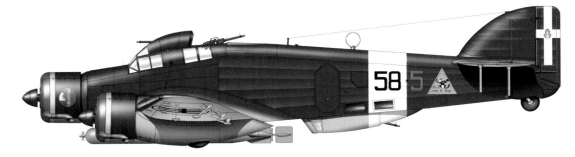

Savoia Marchetti S.79, 58-5, 58^ Squadriglia, 32º Gruppo, 10º Stormo, Sicily, Summer 1942

FLEET AIR ARM

Hawker Sea Hurricane Mk.Ib, V7077/H, No. 801 Naval Air Squadron, HMS *Eagle*, 'Operation Pedestal', August 1942

Fairey Fulmar Mk.II, X8812, No 809 Naval Air squadron, HMS *Victorious*, Operation Pedestal, August 1942. Its crew were credited with one Ju88 shot down and another probable on 11-12 August

Grumman Martlet Mk.II, AM968/8M, flown by Sub Lt J.A. Cotching, No 806 Naval Air Squadron, HMS *Indomitable*, Operation Pedestal, August 1942. Cotching shot down a S79 and a Re2001 on 12 August during this operation, making him the most successful Martlet pilot of the Fleet Air Arm

ROYAL AIR FORCE

Spitfire Vb, EP140/T-M of 249 Squadron, Ta' Qali, Malta, August 1942.

Bristol Beaufighter Mk.IC, TA483, No 248 Squadron, Ta' Qali, Malta, August 1942

Artwork by Richard J. Caruana

THE END OF A FAMOUS SHIP

Ohio is towed stern first from Kalkara Creek on the morning of 19 September, 1946, to be sunk 10 miles off Malta by explosive charges and gunfire from H.M.S. *Virago*

Ohio finally sinks. Her after section had served as Headquarters for the Royal Yugoslav Navy while lying in Kalkara Creek

A model of *Ohio* by Edward Wyatt at the National War Museum in Valletta

A special collectors' model sold by FAMM

Left: The 50 cents stamp in the set to commemorate the 50th anniversary of the award of the George Cross, designed by Harry Borg

'OHIO' IN PAINTINGS

The saga of *Ohio* has been the subject for a large number of artists who depicted the various phases of the tanker's ordeal.

Ohio under attack, a dramatic depiction by Edwin Galea

The arrival of the Santa Marija convoy, Paul Camilleri Cauchi, the Cathedral of the Assumption in Victoria, Gozo. Other paintings by the Camilleri Cauchi with the same theme may be found in the St Mary's Parish Church, Qrendi and at the St Mary Society's King George V Band Club, Mqabba.

ROLL OF HONOUR

ROYAL NAVY

H.M.S. CAIRO

BYE	Alfred W	Stoker Petty Officer
COMBEN	Stephen C	Act/Leading Stoker
CRAGO	Alfred C	Marine
DALLING	Reginald A	Marine
DURNFORD	Laurence G	Marine
EARNSHAW	Joseph	Stoker Petty Officer
GOMES	Alfred F	Cook (S)
HADLOW	Thomas	Marine
HALSEY	William A	Able Seaman
HENDERSON	William	Marine
HUTCHINSON	Alexander	Gunner RA
HUTT	Edwin A	Leading Stoker
LAMB	Frank B	Leading Stoker
LAMBERT	Harry J	Stoker 1st Cl
LEDDY	William P	Leading Steward
MACKAY	Charles	Leading Stoker
MITCHELL	Walter L	Ordinary Seaman
MITTENS	Richard S A	Marine
MULLINEUX	Richard	Corporal
REDMAN	William C	Marine
SLARK	Kenneth J	Marine
WALLACE	Samuel	Marine
WELLINGS	George H	Sergeant
WHALE	William E	Marine
WRIGHT	Norman A	CPO Stoker

H.M.S. EAGLE

ANDERSON	Sydney	Able Seaman
ASKEW	Alfred J	Signalman
ATKINSON	Edward J	Able Seaman
ATKINSON	Eric S	Stoker Petty Officer
BAGGETT	Alfred R E	Able Seaman
BAKER	Thomas W	Able Seaman 3rd Cl
BALDWIN	Edward G	Shipwright
BARDEN	John T H	CPO Cook (S)
BARRETT	Arthur R G	ERA 3rd Cl
BAYNES	Thomas J A	Stoker 1st Cl
BOND	Arthur J	CPO Stoker
BROOKS	Ernest	Act/Leading Stoker
BROWN	John W	Supply CPO

BRUNTON	Louis W L	Stoker 1st Cl
BUTCHER	Benjamin	Act/Leading Stoker
BUTLER	Sidney C	Ordinary Seaman
CALLINGHAM	William O	Able Seaman
CLARK	John M	Act/Leading Stoker
COOMBES	Ronald C	Shipwright 4th Cl
COX	John A	Musician
COYNE	Daniel P	Stoker 2nd Cl
CREESE	Herbert	Marine
CUTLAND	Percy G	Chief Shipwright
DACRE	Albert R P	Cpl. Marine
DAGNELL	Bertie R	Leading Seaman
DAINE	Harold B	Stoker 2nd Cl
DARLEY	Fred	ERA
DAVIDSON	John H C	Ordinary Seaman
DAVIES	William	Assistant Steward
DAVIS	Fredrick T	Stoker Petty Officer
DAWSON	Oscar N	Stoker 1st Cl
DIXON	Gordon C	Ordinary Seaman
DONNELL	Charles M	Ordinary Seaman
DONNELLY	Henry	Ordinary Seaman
EASON	Jack	Ordinary Seaman
EDWARDS	Robert G	Stoker 1st Cl
EGGINGTON	John H C	Steward
FARE	Nelson V	Act/Leading Stoker
FENSHAW	Colin A	Musician
FITTON	Donald	Musician
GEMMELL	Alfred	Ordinary Seaman
GOULDING	Thomas J	ERA
GRAINGER	George T	Sick Berth Attendant
GRANGER	Roy	Marine
GRANT	Ronald G	Act/Leading Stoker
GRAY	Henry	Able Seaman
HAITHWAITE	Leonard A	Odinance Artificer
HALL	Robert	Stoker 1st Cl
HAMILTON	William J	Stoker 1st Cl
HANDLEY	Henry G W	Stoker 2nd Cl
HANDS	William A	Marine
HARGEST	William H	Ty/Lieutenant (E)
HANKEY	Michael	Sub Lieutenant (A)
HARTLEY	Wilfred C	Musician
HARVEY	John D	Act/Stoker Petty officer
HARTWOOD	Douglas M	Joiner 2nd Cl
HAYWARD	Bertram C	Telegraphist
HEARNE	Joseph P	Ordinary Seaman
HEELEY	William A	Leading Air Fitter
HEYMAN	George	Stoker 2nd Cl
HILL	John	ERA 4th Cl
HOLLAND	Albert R P	Stoker Petty Officer
HOOPER	Reginald	Ordinary Seaman

HUDSON	Alfred J	Air Fitter (E)
HUMPHRIES	Stanley L	Musician
HUNTER	Thomas S	Stoker 2nd Cl
JERRED	Ronald J	Ordinary Seaman
JONES	James H	Stoker 1st Cl
JONES	Percival C	Officer's Cook 1st Cl
JUDD	Noel A J	Stoker 2nd Cl
KANE	John M	Ordinary Seaman
LAW	Alec A	Supply Assistant
LAW	Alexander	Ordinary Seaman
LAWSON	John G	Steward
LETT	Ronald F	EA4th Cl
LEVETT	John H	Ordinary Seaman
LILLEY	Arnold L	Stoker 1st Cl
LLEWELLYN	William H	Able Seaman
LUNNON	Kenneth A R	Marine
MADDICKS	William G	Able Seaman
MANDEVILLE	Geoffrey F	Commander (E)
MARSH	Clarence	CPO Stoker
MASON	John	CPO Stoker
MAYLAND	Arthur R	Act/LAM (E)
MACCARRON	Bernard	Act/Leading Stoker
McDONALD	Arnold	Stoker 1st Cl
McGRATH	Daniel J	Stoker 2nd Cl
McGUCKIN	William C	Stoker 1st Cl
McMAHON	John R	Stoker 2nd Cl
MEAD	William C E	Ordinary Seaman
MERRY	Francis W	Telegraphist
MILES	Harold	Stoker 1st Cl
MILLNE	William A	Musician
MILSON	Robert A	Stoker 1st Cl
MOODY	Cyril G	Stoker 1st Cl
MOORE	James	Stoker 1st Cl
MOREY	Arnold H	Leading Writer 2nd Cl
MORRIS	Stanley J	Stoker 2nd Cl
MOSES	Alfred H	ERA 4th Cl
NICHOLLS	John	Stoker 2nd Cl
NORTHEAST	Alfred J C	CPO Steward
OATES	Jack R	Ty/Act/Ldg-Sig
O'BRIEN	Albert J	Supply Assistant
O'MAHONEY	Edmund	Act/ERA 4th Cl
PARKER	Victor R W	Able Seaman
PARSONS	Arthur	Marine
PARTRIDGE	John S	Musician
PEARSON	William S A	Able Seaman
PICKARD	Benjamin	Stoker Petty Officer
POUNDER	Walter C	Stoker 1st Cl
PYCRAFT	James W	Able Seaman
RADLEY	William G	Stoker 1st Cl
RAY	Benjamin	Marine
REED	William	Ordinary Seaman
REGAN	Michael	Marine
REYNOLDS	John B	Stoker 2nd Cl
ROBSON	Daniel S	Stoker 2nd Cl
ROBSON	Stephen	Able Seaman
RUSSELL	Leslie F	Ordinary Seaman
SEARLE	Sidney C	Stoker 2nd Cl
SHEED	Francis	Act/Leading Seaman
SMITH	Albert	Stoker 1st Cl
SMITH	Francis J R	Stoker Petty Officer
SMITH	Ronald W	Musician
SMITH	Thomas H	Shipwright 3rd Cl
SNELGROVE	James	Stoker 1st Cl
SOUTHWELL	James H	CPO Stoker
STEVENS	William H	Sick Berth PO

SYMES	William H	Act/Leading Stoker
TAYLOR	Albert	Able Seaman
TAYLOR	James	ERA 4th Cl
TAYLOR	James	Stoker 2nd Cl
THOMPSON	Edward	Stoker 2nd Cl
THOMPSON	John A	Chief Mechanician
TIERNEY	Patrick G	Steward
TILLER	James A	Petty Officer
TINGLE	Arthur G	Leading Cook (O)
TRORY	William E	Stoker 1st Cl
TWIGG	Joseph	Stoker 2nd Cl
TYRRELL	Lawrence W	Air Mechanic 1st Cl (O)
URWIN	Joseph	Act/Joiner NAAFI 4th Cl
VAGGERS	Denys J	Canteen Assistant
VENVELL	Thomas E	Chief Painter
WADE	William	Ordinary Seaman
WAITE	John H	Chief Ord Art 2nd Cl
WARD	Frank	Steward
WARREN	Edward	Yeoman of Signals
WAUGH	David	Able Seaman
WEAD	James R	Act/Leading Stoker
WELCH	Reginald G	Able Seaman
WELCH	Wilfred R	Able Seaman
WHITE	Dudley N	Act/Able Seaman
WHITE	William C	Able Seaman
WILLIAMS	Charles V	Act/ERA 4th Cl
WILSON	Edward R	Petty Officer
WITCHELL	Desmond T	Musician
WITHERS	Reuben	Ldg SBA
WONDERLEY	John J	Able Seaman
WOOD	Laurence H	Ordinary Seaman
WREN	Jack	Stoker 1st Cl

H.M.S. FORESIGHT

EVANS	Harry R	Lieutenant
JONES	C W	Leading Seaman
MELLORS	Stanley	Stoker 1st Cl
SHELLEY	Samuel B	Act/Petty Officer
WOODS	Victor	Able Seaman

H.M.S. INDOMITABLE

AHEARNE	John P	Marine
ARLOW	Henry	Marine
BAILEY	Edward J	Steward
BIDWELL	Leonard J	Ty/Corporal
BINNS	James W	Marine
BLACKER	Charles E	Steward
BRAY	John C	Steward
CASS	Frank	Steward
CLARK	Henry	Marine
CRUIKSHANK	John I	Ty/Sub Lieutenant
CUNLIFFE-OWEN	Hugo L	Ty/Sub Lieutenant
DOWNING	George E	Air mechanic
FARROW	Dennis W	Marine

FRANKPITT	James	Ty/Corporal
FRASER	David	Marine
GARDNER	Raymond	Marine
GOLDBOURN	Alfred G	Marine
GOURLEY	Robert G	Ty/Sgt Royal Marines
GRAY	Frederick L A	Act/leading Artificer
GREENWOOD	Kenneth G	Ty/Corporal
HEMPSTEAD	Leslie G	Leading Steward
JOHNSTON	Robert L	Lieutenant
JUDD	Francis E C	Lieut Commander
LINDLEY	Ernest	Air Mech 1st Cl (A)
LINDSAY	William C	Air Mech 2nd Cl
LUCAS	John M	Sub Lieutenant
MAXFIELD	George A	Able Seaman
McCHEYNE	George	Marine
MEASURES	George F	Ty/Lieutenant (A)
PARK	Richard B	Lieutenant (A)
PATTEN	Harold Y	Marine
PROTHEROE	William L	Ty/Sub Lieutenant (A)
RICHARDSON	William B	Leading Writer
ROWSELL	Leslie M	Marine
RYAN	Daniel W	Marine
SAINSBURY	John M	LAM (O)
SCOTT	Hugh K	Marine
SIMPKINS	Henry G	Marine (Pens)
SQUIRES	Francis A	Air Mechanic (A)
STEWART	William H	Steward
SUMMERS	Harold E G	Colour Sergeant
TANNER	George A	Paymaster Lieutenant
VASEY	Frank	Act/Joiner 4th Cl
VENABLES	John H	Act/Leading Stoker
WELCH	Victor	Marine
WILDE	Reginald S	Able Seaman
WILLIAMS	Leonard C	Lieutenant
WILLIAMSON	Andrew	Marine
WOOD	Joseph M	Sergeant

H.M.S. KENYA

EVANS	Harold	Able Seaman
JONES	Herbert E C	Able Seaman
PAYNE	William H	Ty/Leading Seaman

H.M.S. MANCHESTER

COYLE	James H	Stoker
DUNNING	Thomas W F	Petty Officer
FRANKLAND	Leonard M	Py/Ty/Sub Lieut (E)
GODDEN	Leslie J	Act/Leading Stoker
HODGKINSON	Francis R	Stoker 1st Cl
NOBLE	William H	Stoker 1st Cl
POWIS	William A	Act/Stoker PO
SMITH	Charles F	Chief Mechanic
TOOGOOD	William	Act/ERA 4th Cl
WHITEHEAD	Ronald G	Able Seaman
TURNER	Bert	Stoker

H.M.S. NIGERIA

ALSOP	Christopher	Able Seaman
ARIS	John C	Ordinary Telegraphist
ARMSTRONG	Kenneth	Ordinary Seaman
BETTS	Charles G	Act/Ldg Telegraphist
BOX	John T	Able Seaman
BOYCE	Gordon C	Ordinary Telegraphist
BRAWN	Cecil G	Ty/Petty officer
BRAY	Eric N	Able Seaman
BURNS	Edgar E	Able Seaman
CASTLE	William E A	Able Seaman
CLARKE	John A	Musician
COLEMAN	Herbert E C	Able Seaman
CONN	Frederick W J	Musician
COOTE	Eric H	Able Seaman
COXON	Kenneth N	Telegraphist
CULVER	Eric R	Able Seaman
EBBAGE	Herbert T	Leading Seaman
FOX	Ernest	Able Seaman
GROSE	Henry	Ordinary Seaman
HART	Reginald T	Able Seaman
HOARE	James	Able Seaman
INGOLDBY	Patrick R	Midshipman
IRVING	Norman	Able Seaman
ISAAC	Douglas J	Able Seaman
JAMES	Gordon P	Stoker 2nd Cl
JOHNSTONE	Cecil F	Ordinary Seaman
JONES	Arthur L	CPO Stoker
KER	Claude B	Midshipman
LEBBING	Clifford H	Able Seaman
MARTINDALE	John T	Ordinary Seaman
MARTYR	Alfred A	Warrant Electrician
MCINNES	James F	Ordinary Seaman
MOREY	William C	Musician
PAGE	Albert R	Supply Assistant
PERRY	Alfred J	Petty Officer
PHILLIPS	Jack A	Musician
POWELL	Richard	Band Corporal
RAY	William D G	Musician
REEVES	Arthur W	Able Seaman
RIDOUT	Albert E	Bandmaster 1st Cl
ROBERTS	Harry G	Able Seaman
ROBINSON	George W A	Leading Telegraphist
ROPE	Aron	Musician
SKOYLES	Henry	Petty Officer
SMITH	Arthur S	Stoker 1st Cl
TUFFILL	John D	Midshipman
WALLER	Herbert A	Able Seaman
WALTER	Arthur V	Musician
WICKS	Thomas A	Able Seaman
WILEY	Edmund	Ty/Act/Ldg Sea
WILKINSON	Cyril	Ordinary Seaman
WILSON	John McE	Able Seaman

H.M.S. VICTORIOUS

CHURCHILL	Robert A F	Lieutenant
EVANS	Charles J	Ty/Sub Lieutenant (A)
NIHILL	John H O'C	Ty/Sub Lieutenant (A)
NUNN	Alan	Lieutenant (A)
REGAN	Walter R	Ty/Act/Ldg Airman
STEWART	John	Ty/Act/Ldg Airman

MERCHANT NAVY

BRISBANE STAR

CORFIELD	E	Greaser

CLAN FERGUSON

ALLSON	A	Apprentice
ANDERSON	J	Greaser
BEAVAN	H E	F and T
BLAIR	A	3rd Engineer
BRUCE	H G	Surgeon
CONNELL	R	F and T
CRAWFORD	W	F and T
GRANT	W McL	6th Engineer
HOLLYWOOD	J	Greaser
McCRORY	W J	1st Radio Officer
RYAN	M	F and T
STEWART	A	Fireman
WILDE	J R	Chief Engineer

DEUCALION

HUTCHINSON	A	Gunner

GLENORCHY

COWLEY	E E	2nd Engineer
FLETCHER	C	Greaser
FOREMAN	T W	Junior Engineer
LESLIE	G.	Master
McQUILLIAM	W	Greaser

SEAL	Herbert R	Gunner
THREFALL	T W	Chief Engineer
WOOD	J W	Junior Engineer

MELBOURNE STAR

BACHE	Harold	Bombardier
GILPIN	William G	Able Seaman
INCE	Howard R	2nd Lieutenant
STEWART	John	Gunner
TURNER	John	Gunner

OHIO

BROWN	Peter	Gunner

SANTA ELISA

FAIRCLOUGH	Thomas	Gunner
TAYLOR	James G	Gunner

WAIMARAMA

BENHAM	George	Gunner
BOND	Rupert	Gunner
BROWN	Lewis C	Gunner
CHITTY	John G	Lance Bombardier
COLLINS	Ira A	Gunner
CREEN	Joseph	Gunner
CROOKSHANK	Alexander O	Second Lieutenant
DEARING	Henry J	Ty/Act/Ldg Seaman
FENSOME	Dennis C J	Signalman
HAWTHORN	Walter G V	Act/Yeoman of Signals
HILL	Thomas	Act/Able Seaman
HITCH	Charles W	Act/Able Seaman
HUFTON	Fredrick H J	Signalman
JOHNSON	William H	Act/Able Seaman
JORDAN	Charles F	Act/Able Seaman
KELLAWAY	Henry C	Act/Able Seaman
MORROW	Victor J	Able Seaman
ORMEROD	Jack	Act/Able Seaman
TAYLOR	Sidney H	Gunner
THOMAS	Edward J	Bombardier
TWIST	Thomas S	Lance Sergeant
WITHERS	John S M	Lieutenant
WREFORD	Arthur J	Gunner

ROYAL AIR FORCE

SMITH	Jerrold	Pilot Officer RCAF
BUNTINE	Robert	Flight Sergeant RAAF
TUNNER	John Harold	Flight Sergeant RNZAF
JAY	David Joseph	Pilot RCAF

The only casualty of Operation Pedestal buried in Malta, at the Capuccini Naval Cemetery at Kalkara was Stoker 1st Class B. Turner of H.M.S. *Manchester*

Explanation of Amount of the accompanying Payable Order in favour of Messrs. MR. FREDERICK T. POUCH.

If any enquiry respecting this payment is necessary, please quote the No. and Date of the Payable Order and return this form to the Director of Navy Accounts, ADMIRALTY, BATH.

	£	s.	d.	
O/Tx 271170. Ord. Tel.	2	12	6	Award for assistance rendered to S.S. "Ohio" by H.M.S. "Bramham" on 13 - 15.8.42.
CARRIED FORWARD				

D.N.A. Form—No. 174. (D.N.A. 4432/34)   DNA 3A/S S.B .122.   (SO106) Wt. 15177/4054 200m/6/43 12 S.L.S.S. Ld. E Gp. 705(2)

The crews of the destroyers which had towed *Ohio* were later awarded salvage money –£2 12s. 6d. each

THE STAMPS

The 88 stamps commemorating the 70th Anniversary of Operation Pedestal are reproduced on 11 colourful sheets. The face value is 26 cents per stamp.

THE ARTIST

Following on the 20 stamp set "Malta Buses - The End of an Era", Maltapost has planned a much bigger project – a record-breaking set to mark the 70th year of Operation Pedestal.

The simple question "Do you know how to draw ships?" went beyond what I could possibly dream or imagine!

After a draft painting was approved, a very tight deadline was set to portray 88 vessels – the total number of ships that in some way or another, took part in what might have possibly been the most important convoy of WW2: Operation Pedestal. From aircraft carriers to destroyers and to fleet oilers and submarines, from corvettes to mine sweepers to motor launches – all protecting the defenceless merchant ships and their valuable cargo from Gibraltar to Malta!

Pictures of the actual vessels are scarce and hard to find – so identifying the classes and history of each vessel was critical in order to be as correct and accurate as possible. Reference was also made to several models and books at the archives of the Maritime Museum at Vittoriosa, and film footage in order to portray the best detail and to be both technically and historically correct. The pennant numbers were omitted in order to keep secret the movements of the warships.

Internet based 3D maps were also used to study the port of Gibraltar and wartime pictures of the Grand Harbour were studied. Weather and sea conditions were noted from several seamen's stories and logs found on the net.

In the paintings, the actual vessels were portrayed and grouped in different positions. These depended on whether the vessel returned to Gibraltar after escorting the convoy up to near Malta, made it into harbour or else was sunk. I shied away from delivering full naval paintings but focused primarily on the vessel as much as possible.

After the final design was finished, the drawings were once again studied by maritime and period specialists to point out anomalies and correct them if need be.

I must say that apart from the actual commissioning of this project, researching and preparing for this project was a totally new and exciting experience for me, as it helped me relive in great detail what our forefathers went through 70 years ago and the courage of the naval sailors and the merchant seamen.

Cedric Galea Pirotta

OPERATION PEDESTAL: THE NAVAL CONVOY
THE MERCHANT SHIPS

Almeria Lykes

Brisbane Star

Clan Ferguson

Deucalion

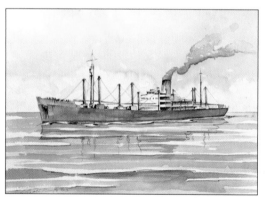

Dorset

Empire Hope

Glenorchy

Melbourne Star

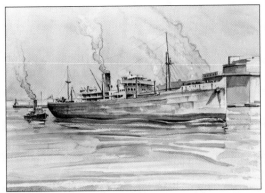

Port Chalmers

Rochester Castle

Santa Elisa

Waimarama

Wairangi

Ohio

FORCE Z

H.M.S. Nelson

H.M.S. Rodney

H.M.S. Victorious

H.M.S. Indomitable

H.M.S. Eagle

H.M.S. Phoebe

H.M.S. Sirius

H.M.S. Charybdis

H.M.S. Laforey

H.M.S. Lightning

H.M.S. Lookout

H.M.S. Quentin

H.M.S. Somali

H.M.S. Eskimo

H.M.S. Tartar

H.M.S. Ithuriel

H.M.S. Antelope

H.M.S. Wishart

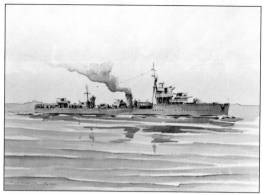

H.M.S. Vansittart

H.M.S. Westcott

H.M.S. Westler

H.M.S. Zetland

H.M.S. Wilton

FORCE X

H.M.S. Nigeria

H.M.S. Kenya

H.M.S. Manchester

H.M.S. Cairo

H.M.S. Ashanti

H.M.S. Bicester

H.M.S. Bramham

H.M.S. Derwent

H.M.S. Foresight

H.M.S. Fury

H.M.S. Icarus

H.M.S. Intrepid

H.M.S. Ledbury

H.M.S. Pathfinder

H.M.S. Penn

FORCE Y

H.M.S. Badsworth

H.M.S. Matchless

OPERATION BELLOWS

H.M.S. Furious

H.M.S. Keppel

H.M.S. Malcolm

H.M.S. Amazon

H.M.S. Venomous

H.M.S. Wolverine

H.M.S. Vidette

CORVETTES

H.M.S. Jonquil

H.M.S. Geranium

H.M.S. Spiraea

H.M.S. Coltsfoot

FLEET OILERS

Brown Ranger

Dingledale

MALTA FORCE

Speedy

Rye

Hebe

Hythe

ML 121

ML 126

ML 134

ML 135

ML 168

ML 459

ML 462

TUGS

Jaunty

Salvonia

SUBMARINES

H.M.S. Unbroken

H.M.S. Safari

H.M.S. Ultimatum

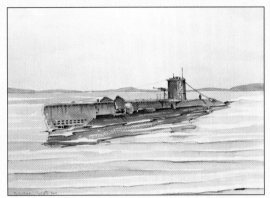

H.M.S. Unruffled

H.M.S. Utmost

H.M.S. United

H.M.S. Una

H.M.S. P222

The Siege Bell Memorial was designed by sculptor Michael Sandle

AUTHOR'S NOTE

I am indebted to several persons and organizations. Writing and compiling this publication has been a race against time as I was approached by Maltapost a few weeks before the deadline of 15 August and as a member of the Stamp Design Board for over 30 years until 2008 I could not refuse. Primary thanks go to Simon Cusens who readily made available his vast array of documents, photographs, personal stories and memorabilia, as well as his advice. His archives on the operation are voluminous and unique.

The Malta War Museum Association let me have the relevant photographs of the operation from their vast collection of over 12,000 photographs of Malta during World War Two. Some of these reproduced in the book have come from the Imperial War Museum, London.

Many individuals have helped, including Joe Caruana with his vast knowledge of the Royal Navy during the war in the Mediterranean. Also Tim Lewin, son of Admiral of the Fleet Lord Terence Lewin. And Jim Hutchinson of H.M.S. *Phoebe* for the designs of the convoy dispositions, and Richard J. Caruana who designed the aircraft involved in the operation, specially for this publication. Thanks also to Emmanel Magro-Conti, Senior Curator Heritage Malta, Maritime and Military Collections, and Charles Debono, Curator Heritage Malta, National War Museum. Also to Ray Polidano, Director General Malta Aviation Museum.

The staff of Midsea Books were most courteous starting with Joseph Mizzi, Managing Director, and Edwin Catania, Sales Manager, and most particularly John Busuttil Leaver, the designer, who for some three weeks put up with me as we compiled the pages.

The chairman of Maltapost, Joseph Said, also deserves my thanks for his advice and support. I found help from Edward Pirotta and the staff of the Philatelic Bureau.

Many books were consulted as were websites.

This list is of some of the best publications that have dealt with Operation Pedestal:

PEDESTAL ; Peter C. Smith

MALTA CONVOY 1940-43: Richard Woodman

AT ALL COSTS: Sam Moses

LE AZIONI NAVALI IN MEDITERRANEO : Ufficio Storico della Marina Militare

LA PARTECIPAZIONE TEDESCA NELLA GUERRA NAVALE NEL MEDITERRANEO 1940-45.

NAVI E MARINAI ITALIANI NELLA SECONDA GUERRA MONDIALE: Elio Ando'; Erminio Bagnasco

MALTA CONVOY: Peter Shankland and Anthony Hunter

THE WAR AT SEA -1939-45: S.W. Schofield

THE OHIO AND MALTA: Michael Pearson

THE HINGE OF FATE, Vol IV, memoirs: Winston S. Churchill

CHURCHILL AND MALTA: Douglas Austin

THE SPITFIRE YEARS: Christopher Shores, Brian Cull, Frederick Galea

MALTA - DEFIANT AND TRIUMPHANT: E.A.S. Bailey

MALTA: BLITZED BUT NOT BEATEN: Philip Vella.

The operation has frequently been the subject of television documentaries, some very good, a few quite superficial. Many documents are now readily available at the Public Records Office, Kew, and at the Admiralty.

I met many of the veterans who attended the reunion in 2002 and understood the ordeal they went through. The George Cross on the flag of Malta honours them, too. I wrote this book in tribute to them.